# A GUIDE TO

# THE MERRY WIVES OF WINDSOR

# The Shakespeare Handbooks

*Guides available now:*

- Antony and Cleopatra
- As You Like It
- The Comedy of Errors
- Cymbeline
- Hamlet
- Henry IV, Part 1
- Julius Caesar
- King Lear
- Macbeth
- Measure for Measure
- The Merchant of Venice
- The Merry Wives of Windsor
- A Midsummer Night's Dream
- Much Ado About Nothing
- Othello
- Richard II
- Romeo and Juliet
- The Tempest
- Twelfth Night
- The Winter's Tale

*Further titles in preparation.*

The Shakespeare Handbooks

# A Guide to The Merry Wives of Windsor

by Alistair McCallum

Upstart Crow Publications

*First published in 2021 by*
*Upstart Crow Publications*

*Copyright © Alistair McCallum 2021*

*A CIP catalogue record for this book*
*is available from the British Library*

*ISBN  978 1 899747 18 4*


*www.shakespeare-handbooks.com*

# Setting the scene

Shakespeare probably wrote *The Merry Wives of Windsor* in 1597-9, when he was in his early thirties. Having started his career as a novice actor ten years or so before, he was by now the principal playwright for London's leading theatre company; his achievements to date included *Richard II, Romeo and Juliet* and *A Midsummer Night's Dream*. He and his fellow company members were soon to set up the renowned Globe Theatre on the south bank of the Thames.

*The Merry Wives of Windsor* was an immediate success with the theatre-going public. The outsize figure of Falstaff, recently introduced in *Henry IV, Part I*, was already a guaranteed crowd-pleaser; and the play's exuberant, farcical nature and cast of colourful characters ensured its continuing popularity.

In 1642, twenty-six years after Shakespeare's death, civil war was looming, and the London theatres were forced to shut down by decree of the Puritan-dominated Parliament. They remained closed for nearly twenty years: many, including the Globe, were demolished. Even then, however, theatre did not die out altogether. Brief, comical sketches known as 'drolls' – usually adapted from old plays – were presented, often surreptitiously, in taverns and private houses. One of the most popular drolls included scenes from *The Merry Wives of Windsor* featuring Falstaff: it was called *The Bouncing Knight*. And when the theatres were allowed to reopen in 1660, *The Merry Wives of Windsor* was one of the first plays to be staged.

In some ways, *Merry Wives* is unlike any other play by Shakespeare. The setting is contemporary, not historical; the characters are, for the most part, everyday citizens; and the location is domestic small-town England, not a far-flung city or the court of an imaginary ruler.

*"*The Merry Wives of Windsor *is not one of Shakespeare's greatest plays; it lacks stirring poetry and monumental characters ... However, it presents a delightfully picturesque view of 16th-century rural life. An expertly plotted farce that ranges from gentle charm to high hilarity, it deploys a dozen splendid comic characters in a world of solid virtue that is exemplified by its commendable though understated heroines. As such, the play has been appreciated by generations of theatregoers."*

Charles Boyce, *Shakespeare A to Z*, 1990

# A troublesome visitor

Windsor: a pleasant, prosperous small town, twenty miles west of London, surrounded by farms and parkland. For the Pages and the Fords, citizens of the town, life is comfortable and stable. Queen Elizabeth has been on the throne for forty years: and although the Queen and her entourage are regular residents at nearby Windsor Castle, the townsfolk generally go about their lives unaffected by the goings-on at court.

The town's other inhabitants include Caius, a hot-blooded French doctor; his talkative housekeeper, Mistress Quickly; Hugh Evans, a well-meaning but incomprehensible Welsh clergyman, given the respectful title Sir Hugh; and the hearty, affable host of the local inn. Among the town's temporary residents are Justice Shallow, a self-important magistrate from Gloucestershire, and his dim-witted young relative Slender.

One visitor in particular, however, threatens to disrupt the harmony of everyday life in Windsor: an impoverished aristocrat from London, disreputable, gross and utterly shameless, his name is Sir John Falstaff. He and his shady gang of followers, always on the lookout for easy money, have already committed a number of petty crimes. But Falstaff has a much grander scheme in mind to separate the citizens of Windsor from their money: and he is keen to put it into practice as soon as possible.

# Curtain up

# A lucrative prospect

In a street in Windsor, Robert Shallow, an elderly magistrate, is complaining to the local parson, Hugh Evans. His grievance is with an infamous debauched aristocrat, Sir John Falstaff.

Shallow is determined to see Falstaff punished to the full extent of the law. He is keenly aware of his own importance in the legal world, as is his impressionable young relative Abraham Slender:

| | |
|---|---|
| *Shallow:* | Sir Hugh, persuade me not:[1] I will make a Star Chamber[2] matter of it. If he were twenty Sir John Falstaffs, he shall not abuse Robert Shallow esquire. |
| *Slender:* | In the County of Gloucester, Justice of Peace and Coram.[3] |
| *Shallow:* | Ay, cousin Slender, and Custalorum.[4] |
| *Slender:* | … and a gentleman born, master parson, who writes himself *Armigero*, in any bill, warrant, quittance, or obligation – *Armigero*.[5] |

[1] *don't try to talk me out of it*
[2] *the highest, most powerful court in the country*
[3] *quorum; magistrate whose presence is officially required at certain trials*
[4] *keeper of the local records*
[5] *who can sign legal documents with a Latin title demonstrating that he is a gentleman with his own coat of arms*

Shallow and Slender discuss their family's coat of arms proudly, but their boasts are lost on Sir Hugh, who appears to think that they are talking about clothing. Changing the subject, Sir Hugh offers to help Shallow by mediating in his dispute with Falstaff. However, Shallow is not interested in reconciliation: if he were younger, he claims, he would resolve the matter with his sword.

Sir Hugh, disapproving of violence, steers the conversation to a different topic. He mentions that George Page, a citizen of Windsor, has a daughter named Anne; she would make an excellent wife for young Abraham Slender.

*If he were twenty Sir John Falstaffs ...*

When *The Merry Wives of Windsor* was first performed, Falstaff was already a great favourite following his introduction in Shakespeare's recent and highly successful *Henry IV, Part I.* He had become a well-known figure both to courtly audiences and to those at the public open-air theatres:

"*Shakespeare knew what he was doing in beginning as he did. For an audience familiar with* Henry IV, Part I *the mere mention of Falstaff in the first speech would have been full of promise, catching their attention at once – a matter of prime importance on the open stage of the Elizabethan theatre, where there were no lights to go down.*"

G. R. Hibbard, Commentary on the Penguin Classics edition of *The Merry Wives of Windsor*, 1973

Sir Hugh's heavy Welsh accent and convoluted manner of speaking, along with Slender's slow-wittedness, make communication difficult, but the message is clear. Anne's grandfather has left her a large sum of money which she will inherit when she reaches the age of seventeen:

| | |
|---|---|
| *Slender:* | Mistress Anne Page? She has brown hair, and speaks small[1] like a woman? |
| *Evans:* | It is that ferry person for all the 'orld, as just as you will desire, and seven hundred pounds of moneys, and gold, and silver, is her grandsire upon his death's-bed – Got[2] deliver to a joyful resurrections! – give, when she is able to overtake seventeen years old. It were a goot motion,[3] if we leave our pribbles and prabbles,[4] and desire a marriage between Master Abraham and Mistress Anne Page. |
| *Slender:* | Did her grandsire leave her seven hundred pound? |
| *Evans:* | Ay, and her father is make her a petter penny.[5] |

[1] *with a quiet, high-pitched voice*
[2] *God*
[3] *good idea*
[4] *squabbles, petty arguments*
[5] *will provide her with even more money*

Shallow agrees that the marriage would be very advantageous, and suggests that they speak to Master Page. As it happens, the three of them are outside Page's house at the moment; moreover, Falstaff is currently a guest with the Page household. Urging Shallow to keep his temper despite his quarrel with Sir John, the parson knocks at the door.

## An invitation to dinner

George Page greets his visitors. Before inviting them in, he mentions to Shallow that he is aware of Falstaff's misdemeanours, and hopes to smooth things over between them. At this moment, however, Falstaff himself emerges from Page's house. He dismisses Shallow's accusations abruptly:

| | |
|---|---|
| *Falstaff:* | Now, Master Shallow, you'll complain of me to the King? |
| *Shallow:* | Knight, you have beaten my men, killed my deer and broke open my lodge.[1] ... This shall be answered.[2] |
| *Falstaff:* | I will answer it straight: I have done all this. That is now answered. |

[1] *broken into my gamekeeper's cottage*
[2] *accounted for, examined in a court of law*

It emerges that Falstaff's unruly companions have also been disrupting life in Windsor. The three of them have robbed Slender, adding insult to injury:

| | |
|---|---|
| *Falstaff:* | ... Slender, I broke your head. What matter have you against me? |
| *Slender:* | Marry, sir, I have matter in my head against you, and against your cony-catching rascals,[1] Bardolph, Nim and Pistol. They carried me to the tavern and made me drunk, and afterward picked my pocket. |

[1] *literally, rabbit catchers; con men, cheats*

*... your cony-catching rascals ...*

Crime was rife in the towns and cities of Elizabethan England, and policing was limited and ineffective. Public places such as markets, fairs and inns were plagued by a bewildering array of crooks, fraudsters and thieves, frequently working in teams. The sheer diversity of the criminal underworld is reflected in the vocabulary of the time:

*foist*: a pickpocket who often stalked victims and used elaborate distraction techniques

*nip*: a thief who cut through purse strings with a *cuttle-bung* (small knife)

*gull, cony, cousin*: potential victim

*barnacle*: accomplice who created a diversion during a gambling session to facilitate cheating

*fullams, bristles, cinque-deuces*: types of loaded dice

*hooker, angler, curber*: thieves who used long hooked poles to steal curtains or other items through open windows

*whipjack*: fraudulent beggar carrying a counterfeit document stating that he had been involved in a shipwreck

The three ruffians address Slender threateningly. Sir Hugh tries to calm the situation, promising that he, along with two other citizens of Windsor, will arbitrate in the dispute. Falstaff asks his companions whether they are guilty of stealing Slender's money, and they all proclaim their innocence. Unable to remember exactly what happened, Slender vows to be more careful in the future. The parson approves:

| | |
|---|---|
| *Slender:* | I'll ne'er be drunk whilst I live again, but in honest, civil, godly company, for this trick. If I be drunk, I'll be drunk with those that have the fear of God, and not with drunken knaves. |
| *Evans:* | So Got 'udge me,[1] that is a virtuous mind. |

[1] *as God is my judge*

Page's wife Meg now comes out to greet the visitors, along with her daughter Anne and her friend Mistress Ford. Page urges everyone to come indoors and join his family for dinner.

The assembled company enters Page's house: but young Slender, overcome with anxiety at the sight of his prospective fiancée Anne Page, remains outside. Alarmed at the thought of having to make conversation with her, he asks his servant Simple for help. Perhaps a book of love poetry will help or, failing that, a collection of witty sayings:

> Slender:     I had rather than forty shillings I had my book of *Songs and Sonnets* here.
> [*enter Simple*]
> How now, Simple, where have you been? I must wait on myself, must I? You have not the *Book of Riddles* about you?

Shallow and Sir Hugh come out of Page's house, and urge Slender to join them inside. They are keen to arrange a formal engagement between the young man and the soon-to-be wealthy Anne Page, but it is not clear whether the slow-witted Slender understands what is expected of him, despite his obedient answers. Sir Hugh's obscure turn of phrase does not help:

> Evans:     But can you affection the 'oman? Let us command to know that of your mouth, or of your lips – for diverse philosophers hold that the lips is parcel of the mouth. Therefore, precisely, can you carry your good will to the maid?
> Shallow:     Cousin Abraham Slender, can you love her?
> Slender:     I hope, sir, I will do as it shall become one that would do reason.
> Evans:     Nay, Got's lords and his ladies, you must speak possitable[1] ...

> [1] *positively*

Eventually Slender promises that he will marry the girl. He suggests, in his clumsy manner, that an affectionate relationship may eventually develop between them:

*Slender:*   I will marry her, sir, at your request. But if there be no great love in the beginning, yet heaven may decrease [1] it upon better acquaintance, when we are married, and have more occasion to know one another. I hope upon familiarity will grow more contempt.[2] But if you say marry her, I will marry her ...

[1] *increase*
[2] *content*

At this point Anne Page herself comes out of the house, and asks the three men to join them for dinner. Shallow and Sir Hugh go inside, but Slender again lingers nervously outside the door. He attempts unsuccessfully to engage Anne in conversation. Sending his servant Simple away, he remarks that he has to live fairly modestly, at least until he inherits his parents' wealth. Anne, uninterested, repeats that his presence is requested indoors:

*Slender:*   I keep but three men [1] and a boy yet, till my mother be dead. But what though,[2] yet I live like a poor gentleman born.

*Anne:*   I may not go in without your worship: they will not sit till you come.

[1] *I have only three manservants*
[2] *despite that*

Hearing some dogs barking indoors, Slender turns to the subject of bear-baiting, an activity that he loves. Anne does not share his enthusiasm, and is unimpressed by his boast that he has come close to one of the most famous bears in the country:

| | |
|---|---|
| *Slender:* | Be there bears[1] i'the town? |
| *Anne:* | I think there are, sir; I heard them talked of. |
| *Slender:* | I love the sport well ... You are afraid if you see the bear loose, are you not? |
| *Anne:* | Ay indeed, sir. |
| *Slender:* | That's meat and drink to me now. I have seen Sackerson[2] loose twenty times, and have taken him by the chain ... |

[1] *bear-baiting arenas*
[2] *a famous fighting bear*

---

*I have seen Sackerson loose twenty times ...*

The Globe Theatre, owned by Shakespeare's acting company, was situated in Southwark, just outside the City of London. The area was home to many taverns and brothels, as well as a number of theatres. Another attraction was the Bear Garden, where bears, usually chained to a post, would be pitted against ferocious dogs, or taunted by men with whips. Occasionally a bear would break free, causing uproar amongst the audience. Some bears became famous for their resilience and courage, and were given nicknames by regular patrons.

Although the activity seems barbaric now, bear-baiting was hugely popular in Tudor England; Queen Elizabeth, for example, was very keen on it, as had been her father, King Henry VIII. When the activity started to fall out of fashion, official attempts were made to sustain it:

*"... the 'sport', faced with the new craze of the theatre, was in decline. To support it, in 1591, the authorities decreed that no theatrical performances should take place on a Thursday, to give the bear-pits a clear run."*

Nicholas Fogg, *Hidden Shakespeare*, 2013

The awkward exchange is brought to an end when George Page emerges from his house and demands cheerfully that Slender join them for dinner. The young man timidly asks Anne to go in first, while she insists that he should lead the way. Unwilling to cause offence, Slender finally goes in to join the others.

A short while later, Sir Hugh briefly leaves the dinner party to talk to Slender's servant Simple. The parson has thought of someone who may help to bring Slender and Anne Page together. Doctor Caius, a French physician who now lives in Windsor, has a housekeeper, Mistress Quickly: she is a close acquaintance of Anne's, and may be able to persuade the young woman to look favourably on Slender.

The parson has written a note to Mistress Quickly asking for her help. In his usual convoluted way, he instructs Simple to deliver the message:

*Evans:*     … give her this letter. For it is a 'oman that altogether's acquaintance with Mistress Anne Page, and the letter is to desire, and require her, to solicit your master's [1] desires to Mistress Anne Page. I pray you be gone; I will make an end of my dinner, there's pippins [2] and cheese to come.

[1] *Slender's*
[2] *apples*

# Falstaff's scheme

Despite his aristocratic status, Sir John Falstaff is perennially short of money. He and his three attendants are staying at the Garter Inn in Windsor, and Falstaff is concerned at the amount he is paying for their board and lodging. To help his finances, the host of the Garter agrees to take on Bardolph, one of Falstaff's companions, to serve in the tavern.

The host makes it clear to his new employee that fleecing the customers is part of the job:

*Host:* ... Let me see thee froth[1] and lime.[2] I am at a word,[3] follow.

*Falstaff:* Bardolph, follow him. A tapster is a good trade: an old cloak makes a new jerkin;[4] a withered servingman,[5] a fresh tapster. Go, adieu.

[1] *make sure there is a large head of foam, to reduce the amount of beer served*
[2] *adulterate old, sour wine to make it more palatable*
[3] *I am as good as my word; I'll keep my promise*
[4] *jacket*
[5] *attendant, manservant*

When Bardolph is out of earshot, Falstaff remarks that he will not be missed. As a thief, Bardolph was becoming unreliable, he complains:

*Falstaff:* I am glad I am so acquit[1] of this tinderbox.[2] His thefts were too open: his filching was like an unskilful singer, he kept not time.

*Nim:* The good humour[3] is to steal at a minute's rest.[4]

[1] *rid*
[2] *referring to Bardolph's red nose and inflamed complexion*
[3] *the right method*
[4] *quickly, and at just the right time, like taking a brief pause during a piece of music*

Falstaff tells his remaining two companions, Nim and Pistol, that he has a plan to get himself out of his current financial difficulties. Brushing aside Pistol's jibe at his bloated belly, he explains that Mistress Ford, a friend of the Page family, is clearly attracted to him:

*Falstaff:*    My honest lads, I will tell you what I am about.
*Pistol:*    Two yards, and more.
*Falstaff:*    No quips now, Pistol. – Indeed I am in the waist two yards about, but I am now about no waste: I am about thrift. Briefly, I do mean to make love to [1] Ford's wife. I spy entertainment in her: [2] she discourses, she carves, [3] she gives the leer of invitation.

[1] *pursue, make advances to*
[2] *I can tell that she responds to my company*
[3] *she talks to me, and treats me hospitably*

Ford is a wealthy man, and it is rumoured that his wife controls the family's money. Falstaff reveals that, as the first step in his pursuit of Mistress Ford, he has written a letter ready to be delivered to her. However, she is not his only target. Mistress Page, too, seems to find him irresistible:

*Falstaff:*    O, she did so course o'er my exteriors, [1] with such a greedy intention, that the appetite of her eye did seem to scorch me up like a burning glass. [2]

[1] *run her eye over my features*
[2] *like a magnifying glass concentrating the sun's rays*

Falstaff intends to pursue Mistress Page too, and has a further letter prepared for her. He revels in the prospect of gaining access to her wealth, as well as that of Mistress Ford:

*Falstaff:*    … she is a region in Guiana, all gold and bounty. I will be cheaters [1] to them both, and they shall be exchequers [2] to me. They shall be my East and West Indies, and I will trade to them both.

[1] *official in charge of royal estates*
[2] *treasuries, banks*

Handing one letter to Nim, and the other to Pistol, Falstaff instructs them to deliver the letters to the two wives straight away. The future looks bright for all three of them, he declares excitedly. However, his companions' reaction comes as a shock: they both feel that acting as a go-between is beneath their dignity, and flatly refuse to take part in their master's plan.

Giving the letters instead to Robin, his young page-boy, Falstaff angrily dismisses his two attendants:

Falstaff:    Rogues, hence, avaunt![1] Vanish like hailstones, go!
              Trudge, plod away o'th' hoof, seek shelter, pack!

[1] be gone

Falstaff storms away. Nim and Pistol, resentful at being rejected so high-handedly, decide to take revenge by revealing Falstaff's plans to the two women's husbands. Pistol becomes poetic as he envisages breaking the news to Master Page, and Nim vows to persuade Master Ford to take drastic action:

Nim:    I will discuss the humour[1] of this love to Ford.
Pistol:    And I to Page shall eke[2] unfold
         How Falstaff, varlet vile,
         His dove will prove,[3] his gold will hold,
         And his soft couch defile.[4]
Nim:    My humour shall not cool: I will incense Ford to deal
         with poison, I will possess him with yellowness[5] …

[1] disclose the nature
[2] also
[3] will test the fidelity of his beloved wife
[4] will desecrate his matrimonial bed
[5] jealousy

# An unreliable ally

A visitor has arrived at doctor Caius' house. It is Slender's servant Peter Simple, sent by the parson to enlist the help of the Frenchman's housekeeper Mistress Quickly.

The doctor is not at home at the moment. Mistress Quickly allows Simple into the house, but is uneasy; the doctor is notoriously short-tempered, and is likely to start a quarrel with the young servant. At first, she cannot recall who Slender is, but eventually remembers him, and agrees that he will be a good match for Anne. She promises she will try to persuade Anne to look on him favourably.

The conversation is cut short as doctor Caius comes home unexpectedly. Mistress Quickly hurriedly bundles Simple into a closet and puts on an innocent air, singing to herself as her master comes in. Irascible as ever, the doctor tells her to stop singing, and orders her to fetch a box from the closet. He is in a hurry, and is about to go out again. However, at the last minute he realises that he has forgotten something:

> Caius:      'Od's me, *qu'ai-je oublié?*[1] Dere is some simples[2] in my closet dat I will not for the varld I shall leave behind.
>
> *Mistress Quickly:*   Ay me, he'll find the young man there, and be mad!
>
> [1] *God save me, what have I forgotten?*
> [2] *medicinal herbs*

As Mistress Quickly had feared, the doctor discovers Simple in the closet. He calls furiously for his rapier, but Mistress Quickly manages to calm him down, and he allows Simple to explain why he has come. Hearing about Sir Hugh's plan to bring Slender and Anne Page together, doctor Caius tells Simple to wait while he writes a note for the parson.

It emerges that the doctor himself has designs on the young heiress although, Mistress Quickly implies, she does not return his feelings. The Frenchman is determined to settle the matter by means of a duel:

Mistress Quickly: [aside, to Simple] ... to tell you in your ear, I would have no words of it [1] – my master himself is in love with Mistress Anne Page; but notwithstanding that, I know Anne's mind – that's neither here nor there.

Caius: You, Jack'nape: give-a this letter to Sir Hugh. By gar,[2] it is a shallenge: I will cut his throat in de park, and I will teach a scurvy jackanape priest to meddle or make.[3]

[1] *don't tell anyone else*
[2] *by God*
[3] *interfere*

The renowned 16th-century French surgeon Ambrose Paré had a major influence on the medical and surgical practice of his day. At a time when medicine was unregulated, unscientific and governed largely by beliefs that dated back to Ancient Greece, Paré was a pioneer of treatment based on practical experience, close observation, and logical analysis. He was particularly successful in dealing with battlefield wounds.

Unfortunately, there were plenty of unscrupulous individuals ready to take advantage of the great man's reputation:

"French doctors were much in vogue in the 1590s, with Englishmen pretending to be French in order to exploit the fashion, perhaps inspired by the Parisian physician Ambrose Paré, famed for his sensational writings, who had died in 1590. This was also reflected in the drama of the time, with French doctors, usually comic, appearing frequently ... Dr Caius is quite credible as a pillar of Windsor society."

Kathy Elgin, Programme notes for RSC production of The Merry Wives of Windsor, 1992

Simple hurries away with the letter. The doctor turns to Mistress Quickly accusingly: she had previously assured him that Anne would agree to marry him. Sir Hugh must pay for his attempt to influence Anne, he vows. In his letter, he has nominated the host of the Garter to supervise the planned duel. The housekeeper nervously brushes aside Simple's words as meaningless gossip:

*Caius:*  Do not you tell-a-me dat I shall have Anne Page for myself? By gar, I vill kill de Jack-priest; and I have appointed mine host of the Jarteer to measure our weapon.[1] By gar, I will myself have Anne Page.

*Mistress Quickly:* Sir, the maid loves you, and all shall be well. We must give folks leave to prate, what the good-year![2]

[1] *act as umpire in our duel*
[2] *what the devil, we must expect foolish chatter*

Caius leaves, threatening Mistress Quickly that she will be thrown out of his house if Anne Page will not marry him.

A moment later, another visitor arrives. This time it is Fenton, an aristocratic young gentleman who, like Slender and Caius, has his heart set on marrying Anne Page. He too has been assured by Mistress Quickly that Anne loves him above all other suitors. Fenton asks anxiously whether this is still the case:

*Fenton:*  Shall I do any good, thinkest thou? Shall I not lose my suit?[1]

*Mistress Quickly:* Troth,[2] sir, all is in His hands above. But notwithstanding, Master Fenton, I'll be sworn on a book she loves you.

[1] *fail in my quest to marry Anne*
[2] *truthfully*

Fenton slips some money into Mistress Quickly's hand, urging her again to put in a good word for him when she next sees Anne Page. As he leaves, the housekeeper remarks to herself that – despite her earlier assurances – Fenton's hopes are likely to be dashed:

*Mistress Quickly:* Farewell to your worship. [*exit Fenton*]
Truly an honest gentleman – but Anne loves him not.
For I know Anne's mind as well as another does.

# Comparing notes

The next morning, Anne's mother, Mistress Page, receives a letter. She is taken aback when she realises that it is from an admirer:

> *Mistress Page:* What, have I scaped[1] love-letters in the holiday-time of my beauty,[2] and am I now a subject for them?
>
> [1] *escaped, avoided*
> [2] *when I was young, and at the height of my beauty*

The letter assures her that she and the writer have a great deal in common:

> *You are not young, no more am I: go to,[1] then, there's sympathy.[2] You are merry, so am I: ha, ha, then there's more sympathy. You love sack,[3] and so do I: would you desire better sympathy?[4]*
>
> [1] *come on; you can't deny it*
> [2] *fellow-feeling, similarity*
> [3] *sweet Spanish wine*
> [4] *could we be more alike?*

After declaring his love for Mistress Page, the writer ends with a poetic flourish:

> *By me, thine own true knight,*
> *By day or night,*
> *Or any kind of light,*
> *With all his might,*
> *For thee to fight,*
> > *John Falstaff.*

Mistress Page is outraged at the behaviour of this gross, elderly drunkard whom she has only met a few times. His impudence is intolerable:

> *Mistress Page:* O wicked, wicked world! One that is well-nigh worn to pieces with age, to show himself a young gallant? … How shall I be revenged on him? For revenged I will be, as sure as his guts are made of puddings.

At this moment Mistress Ford comes to join her friend. She is clearly agitated, and Falstaff is to blame. It emerges that she too has received a message from the lascivious old knight. The two women compare their letters, and find that they are virtually identical:

*Mistress Ford:* What tempest, I trow,[1] threw this whale, with so many tuns[2] of oil in his belly, ashore at Windsor? How shall I be revenged on him? I think the best way were to entertain him with hope,[3] till the wicked fire of lust have melted him in his own grease. Did you ever hear the like?

*Mistress Page:* Letter for letter, but that the name of Page and Ford differs!

[1] *I wonder*
[2] *barrels*
[3] *play along with him, keep him interested*

Although the two women feel the same revulsion and anger, Mistress Page cannot help wondering whether she has encouraged Falstaff without realising it. Her friend is horrified at the thought of physical contact with the gluttonous knight:

*Mistress Ford:* What doth he think of us?

*Mistress Page:* Nay, I know not. It makes me almost ready to wrangle with mine own honesty.[1] I'll entertain myself like one that I am not acquainted withal.[2] For, sure, unless he know some strain in me that I know not myself, he would never have boarded[3] me in this fury.[4]

*Mistress Ford:* Boarding, call you it? I'll be sure to keep him above deck.[5]

[1] *question my own integrity*
[2] *I'm forced to think of myself as a stranger*
[3] *approached, attacked (as in naval warfare)*
[4] *so impetuously*
[5] *above the waist*

The two friends decide to play along with Falstaff by pretending to be interested in his amorous advances. With luck, the expense of wooing the two women, along with a lengthy stay at the Garter, will bankrupt him.

Mistress Ford remarks that her husband, who is unnecessarily jealous at the best of times, would be shocked if he became aware of Falstaff's letter. She envies her friend, whose husband is much more easy-going. As they talk, the women's husbands approach. Rather than speak to them, however, the two friends decide to withdraw and plan their revenge against Falstaff:

> *Mistress Ford:* O, that my husband saw this letter! It would give eternal food to his jealousy.
>
> *Mistress Page:* Why, look where he comes; and my good man too – he's as far from jealousy as I am from giving him cause, and that, I hope, is an unmeasurable distance.
>
> *Mistress Ford:* You are the happier woman.
>
> *Mistress Page:* Let's consult together against this greasy [1] knight. Come hither.

[1] *fat; lecherous*

---

The nineteenth-century German revolutionaries Karl Marx and Friedrich Engels, authors of *The Communist Manifesto*, were lifelong admirers of Shakespeare. They both had a deep, detailed knowledge of his plays, and quoted from them frequently. His complex depiction of human behaviour, and of economic and political turbulence, along with the sheer beauty and vitality of his language, placed him, in their eyes, in the very highest rank of literary achievement:

*"There is more life and reality in the first act of* The Merry Wives *than in all of German literature."*

Letter from Friedrich Engels to Karl Marx, December 1873

# Seeds of doubt

Falstaff's two disgruntled followers, Pistol and Nim, have just informed Page and Ford of Sir John's intentions towards their wives. Both husbands are sceptical, though the jealous Ford worries that there may be some truth in the report, and decides that he must speak to Falstaff in person.

Just as Pistol and Nim leave, the two wives return briefly. Mistress Quickly also passes by, on her way to talk to Anne Page; when they catch sight of her, the two wives decide that she can help them with their deception of Falstaff. The three women go together into Page's house.

Left alone, the two husbands discuss the news they have just been given. Page points out that Pistol and Nim are resentful of their dismissal by Falstaff, and are not to be trusted. He has no fears about his wife's conduct. Ford, on the other hand, does not want the dissolute knight anywhere near his wife:

| | |
|---|---|
| *Page:* | If he should intend this voyage [1] toward my wife, I would turn her loose to him,[2] and what he gets more of her than sharp words, let it lie on my head.[3] |
| *Ford:* | I do not misdoubt [4] my wife, but I would be loath to turn them together. A man may be too confident. |

[1] *quest, seduction*
[2] *leave her free to do as she likes*
[3] *it will be my responsibility*
[4] *mistrust*

The exchange is interrupted as a pair of passers-by arrive on the scene. It is the host of the Garter Inn and Justice Shallow, and both men are in high spirits. Doctor Caius has challenged Sir Hugh to a duel, they report: but the host, who is to act as umpire, has given each participant a different meeting-place, so no-one should come to any harm.

Ford briefly takes the host aside to ask him a favour. For his own reasons, he says, he intends to visit Falstaff in disguise at the Garter. He asks the host – with the promise of a generous quantity of wine – to pretend not to know him, and to introduce him under the name of Brook. The host willingly agrees.

Shallow and the host set off to see what happens with the two rivals. Page agrees to come with them, confident that there will be a noisy argument rather than any violence. Ford, now alone, muses on the possibility that his wife may not be completely trustworthy. Either way, he needs to know:

Ford:  Though Page be a secure[1] fool, and stands so firmly on his wife's frailty,[2] yet I cannot put off my opinion so easily. She was in his company[3] at Page's house, and what they made[4] there I know not. Well, I will look further into't ... If I find her honest I lose not my labour.[5] If she be otherwise, 'tis labour well bestowed.

[1]  *over-confident*
[2]  *is so sure of his wife despite her moral weakness*
[3]  *my wife was in Falstaff's company*
[4]  *what they got up to*
[5]  *my efforts won't have been wasted*

# The ladies' man                                               II, ii

Pistol has come to the Garter Inn to try to borrow some money from his ex-employer. Failing that, he warns, he will have to resort to violence and extortion. Falstaff is unmoved. He has often had to use his influence to save Pistol and Nim from imprisonment, he declares angrily, and has even risked his own friendships for their sake:

Falstaff:  I will not lend thee a penny.
Pistol:  Why then, the world's mine oyster,
Which I with sword will open.[1]
Falstaff:  Not a penny. I have been content, sir, you should lay my countenance to pawn;[2] I have grated upon[3] my good friends for three reprieves for you and your coach-fellow Nim, or else you had looked through the grate like a gemini of baboons.[4]

[1]  *I will be forced to use my sword to make my way in the world, just as I use a blade to open an oyster*
[2]  *borrow money from others on the strength of your association with me*
[3]  *pestered, harassed*
[4]  *you would have been left looking through the bars of a prison like a pair of foolish apes*

Falstaff has not forgiven Pistol for his refusal to deliver his letter to Mistress Ford. Even an aristocrat like himself has to put his good name at risk from time to time, he complains; it is ridiculous for a rogue like Pistol, of all people, to cling stubbornly to the idea of honour.

Falstaff's furious onslaught is interrupted as Robin, his page-boy, announces that he has a visitor, and Mistress Quickly enters. She has been sent by Mistresses Page and Ford to persuade Falstaff that they have responded positively to his love-letters.

---

Time and again in Shakespeare we find vivid, striking words and phrases, many coined by the author, that have since become part of the fabric of the English language. In *Merry Wives* alone, for example, we find:

> *the world's mine oyster*
>
> *laughing stock*
>
> *the short and the long of it*
>
> *what the dickens*
>
> *as good luck would have it*

In Shakespeare's time, English was in a state of flux; pronunciation, grammar and spelling were all much more flexible than they are in modern English. This gave the language an energy and inventiveness that still appeals to us:

*"Elizabethan English, alone among the earlier stages of our language, still plays a part in modern intellectual life. Thanks to the English Bible, the prayer-book and Shakespeare, it has never become really obsolete ... Modern English is the fitting medium of an age which leaves little unexplained; while Elizabethan English stands for an age too hasty to analyse what it felt. The one has the virtues of maturity, a logic, uncompromising and clear: the other, a vigour and a felicity, the saving graces of youth."*

A.W. Ward and A. R. Waller, *The Cambridge History of English and American Literature*, 1921

At the mention of Mistress Ford, Falstaff immediately demands to know more. Mistress Quickly, talkative as ever, describes Mistress Ford's reaction to the letter at great length. Falstaff has succeeded in arousing the lady's interest, she claims, where countless others have failed:

*Falstaff:* Well, Mistress Ford – What of her?

*Mistress Quickly:* Why, sir, she's a good creature – Lord, Lord, your worship's a wanton![1] Well, God forgive you, and all of us, I pray –

*Falstaff:* Mistress Ford, come, Mistress Ford.

*Mistress Quickly:* Marry, this is the short and the long of it: you have brought her into such a canary as 'tis wonderful.[2] The best courtier of them all, when the court lay at Windsor, could never have brought her to such a canary – yet there has been knights, and lords, and gentlemen, with their coaches … I warrant you, they could never get an eye-wink[3] of her.

[1] *rascal*
[2] *an incredible quandary, state of confusion*
[3] *flirtatious glance, fluttering of eyelashes*

Falstaff listens impatiently, but is rewarded with some encouraging news. Mistress Ford has arranged an assignation later this very morning:

*Falstaff:* But what says she to me? Be brief, my good she-Mercury.[1]

*Mistress Quickly:* Marry, she hath received your letter, for the which she thanks you a thousand times; and she gives you to notify that her husband will be absence[2] from his house between ten and eleven.

[1] *female version of Mercury, the messenger of the gods*
[2] *absent*

Falstaff promises that he will not miss their rendezvous. Mistress Quickly goes on to mention that she also has a message from Mistress Page, who, like her friend, has become infatuated with the knight. Falstaff protests modestly that he cannot explain why women find him irresistible:

*Mistress Quickly:* ... she bade me tell your worship that her husband is seldom from[1] home, but she hopes there will come a time. I never knew a woman so dote upon a man – surely I think you have charms,[2] la;[3] yes, in truth.

*Falstaff:* Not I, I assure thee. Setting the attraction of my good parts[4] aside, I have no other charms.

[1] *away from*
[2] *magical powers*
[3] *really*
[4] *qualities, attributes*

Falstaff is concerned that the two women may know of each other's intentions, but Mistress Quickly reassures him that they are both very discreet and trustworthy. As she leaves, Falstaff rewards her with a generous sum of money. Robin, the knight's page-boy, is to act as go-between, and he leaves with her.

Pistol, who has been listening quietly in the background, decides that he may be able to profit from Mistress Quickly and her intrigues. He follows her as she leaves the inn.

## A shock for Master Ford

Alone, Falstaff reflects on his success. His ageing body, obese though it may be, is clearly still capable of attracting female attention, and has brought him the prospect of great wealth from his two devoted admirers. His reverie is cut short as another visitor is announced. The caller has asked for a tankard of Spanish wine to be brought up to the room in advance, and Falstaff greets him warmly.

The visitor introduces himself as Brook; in reality, of course, he is Mistress Ford's husband in disguise. Brook hints that he may be able to help Falstaff financially. Money is always useful, Falstaff replies:

*Ford:* ... they say if money go before, all ways do lie open.
*Falstaff:* Money is a good soldier, sir, and will on.[1]

[1] *will always make progress*

Brook produces a large purse to demonstrate that he is in earnest. He then goes on to describe his problem. He is hopelessly in love with a woman by the name of Mistress Ford, he explains, but has had no success with her. He has done everything he can to win her favour, and has bought her countless presents, but she has not shown the slightest degree of interest in him:

Ford:     Briefly, I have pursued her as love hath pursued me, which hath been on the wing of all occasions.[1] But whatsoever I have merited, either in my mind or in my means,[2] meed,[3] I am sure, I have received none – unless experience be a jewel, that I have purchased at an infinite rate ...

      [1] *whenever the opportunity has arisen*
      [2] *whatever efforts I have made, and however much money I have spent*
      [3] *reward, satisfaction*

Falstaff asks what he can do to help. At first, Brook does not answer directly: instead he suggests that, according to rumours, Mistress Ford is not as virtuous or unattainable as she appears. He then goes on to list Sir John's exceptional qualities:

Ford:     ... you are a gentleman of excellent breeding, admirable discourse,[1] of great admittance,[2] authentic in your place and person,[3] generally allowed[4] for your many warlike, courtlike and learned preparations.[5]

      [1] *conversation*
      [2] *having free access to the highest social circles*
      [3] *entitled to respect for your status and character*
      [4] *recognised*
      [5] *scholarly accomplishments*

Finally, he appeals to Falstaff, who is clearly attractive to women, to do everything he can to seduce Mistress Ford. Money is no object, he insists, indicating his purse:

Ford:     There is money: spend it, spend it, spend more, spend
          all I have; only give me so much of your time in
          exchange of it, as to lay an amiable[1] siege to the
          honesty[2] of this Ford's wife. Use your art of wooing,
          win her to consent to you: if any man may, you may as
          soon as any.

          [1] *amorous*
          [2] *virtue, fidelity*

Falstaff is gratified by the visitor's flattery, but puzzled at his request: how will Brook benefit if another man seduces Mistress Ford? Brook explains that, for the time being, the lady is aloof, protected by her apparent respectability. If he can confront her with proof of her infidelity, he reasons, she will have no defence against him:

Ford:     ... I could drive her then from the ward[1] of her purity,
          her reputation, her marriage vow and a thousand other
          her defences, which now are too too strongly embattled
          against me.

          [1] *protection, fortress*

"... *in the mid 1590s when* Merry Wives *was written, the aristocracy was becoming impoverished and turning to trade for finance and to the emerging wealthy middle class for marriage ...* Falstaff *misunderstands his time. He believes his breeding gives him automatic access to the beds of the bourgeoisie. He reckons without their newfound self-confidence and pride; their moral strength built on financial security.*"

Director Bill Alexander, commenting on his 1985
Royal Shakespeare Company production of *The
Merry Wives of Windsor*

Falstaff, delighted with the transaction, takes Brook's purse and shakes his hand. Brook will succeed with Mistress Ford, he promises. Indeed, he reveals, he himself has a romantic assignation with the lady later this morning.

Beneath his disguise, the horrified Ford struggles to remain calm as Sir John boasts that he will both seduce Mistress Ford and use her to gain access to her husband's wealth. He does not even find the woman particularly attractive, he remarks casually:

*Falstaff:* … I shall be with her between ten and eleven, for at that time the jealous rascally knave her husband will be forth.[1] Come you to me at night: you shall know how I speed.[2]

*Ford:* I am blessed in your acquaintance. Do you know Ford, sir?

*Falstaff:* Hang him, poor cuckoldly knave, I know him not. Yet I wrong him to call him poor: they say the jealous wittolly[3] knave hath masses of money, for the which his wife seems to me well-favoured.[4] I will use her as the key of the cuckoldly rogue's coffer …

[1] *away from home*
[2] *make progress, succeed*
[3] *meekly married to an unfaithful wife*
[4] *which makes his wife seem good-looking*

Falstaff assures Brook once again that Mistress Ford will be his; there is no need to be afraid of the woman's husband, whoever he may be. With that, the knight takes his leave.

Ford can contain his fury no longer. Unaware that his wife is playing a trick on Falstaff, he tells himself angrily that his jealousy has been proved to be justified: Page is a fool to be so trusting. Ford resolves to catch his wife with Falstaff and take his revenge:

*Ford:* My wife hath sent to him, the hour is fixed, the match is made: would any man have thought this? … God be praised for my jealousy! Eleven o'clock the hour – I will prevent this, detect[1] my wife, be revenged on Falstaff and laugh at Page. I will about it[2] …

[1] *expose, reveal the truth about*
[2] *make a start, get a move on*

# Violence is averted

In a field near Windsor, doctor Caius is waiting impatiently with his servant John Rugby. He has come to the appointed place for a duel with Sir Hugh, resentful at the parson's attempt to persuade his beloved Anne Page to marry Slender.

The doctor intends to kill his opponent: clutching his rapier restlessly, he orders his servant to pick up his own weapon so that he can demonstrate his technique. Nervous of his master's fiery temper, Rugby is anxious not to cross swords with him, and is relieved to see a group of men approaching.

The four men – the host of the Garter Inn, Justice Shallow, Slender and Master Page – greet the doctor cheerfully. The host claims that they have come to witness the duel, though in reality he has sent the two rivals to different places so that nothing will come of the challenge. When Caius complains that the parson has failed to turn up, Shallow suggests that he has done the right thing:

*Shallow:* He is the wiser man, Master Doctor: he is a curer of souls and you a curer of bodies. If you should fight, you go against the hair [1] of your professions.

[1] *against the grain, contrary to the ideals*

The host instructs his companions to go to Frogmore, a village just outside Windsor; out of earshot of the doctor, he mentions that they will find his rival, Sir Hugh, waiting there.

---

*"The play creates the impression of life in an English provincial town as it is being lived at the moment of the play's first performance ... it retains a contemporary, domestic, and non-aristocratic feel unique in Shakespearean drama."*

Walter Cohen, Introduction to the Norton Shakespeare edition of *The Merry Wives of Windsor*, 1977

---

When the three men have left, the host persuades Caius that his quarrel with the parson is not worth pursuing; instead, he can offer the much more interesting prospect of meeting Anne Page. At this very moment, she is dining at a farmhouse near Frogmore:

*Caius:* By gar, me vill kill de priest, for he speak for a jackanape[1] to Anne Page.

*Host:* Let him die.[2] Sheathe thy impatience. Throw cold water on thy choler.[3] Go about the fields with me through Frogmore. I will bring thee where Mistress Anne Page is, at a farmhouse a-feasting, and thou shalt woo her.

[1] *he has spoken to Anne Page on behalf of that idiot Slender*
[2] *leave him to die of old age*
[3] *anger*

The doctor responds enthusiastically to the idea of meeting Anne. He thanks the host profusely, and the two of them set out towards Frogmore.

# A change of heart III, i

In a field in Frogmore, Sir Hugh, rapier in hand, is waiting for his opponent. Slender's servant Simple is with him, and he instructs the man to look again for doctor Caius, who is late for their encounter. The parson, in a state of agitation, expresses contempt for his rival's profession:

*Evans:* Jeshu pless my soul, how full of cholers I am, and trempling of mind ... I will knog his urinals about his knave's costard[1] when I have good opportunities for the 'ork.

[1] *I will beat the villain around the head with his own urine-collecting bottles*

To lift his spirits, Sir Hugh sings a half-remembered snatch of a love song, mixed with a few words from a psalm. Suddenly, Simple calls out that he has spotted Caius in the distance. At the same time, coming from another direction, Simple's master Slender approaches, along with Shallow and Master Page.

Sir Hugh, guilty at having his rapier drawn in the presence of his friends, hastily takes out his bible and starts reading. The visitors pretend to be unaware of the planned duel. Page is concerned that the ageing clergyman will suffer from the cold:

| | |
|---|---|
| *Shallow:* | What, the sword and the word?[1] Do you study them both, Master Parson? |
| *Page:* | And youthful still – in your doublet and hose,[2] this raw-rheumatic day? |
| *Evans:* | There is reasons and causes for it. |

[1] *sword fighting and the word of God*
[2] *close-fitting jacket and breeches; without a cloak for warmth*

Page and Shallow warn Sir Hugh that doctor Caius is nearby, and appears to be in a ferocious, vengeful mood, although they claim not to know who offended him. Caius now approaches, escorted by the host of the Garter.

Evans and Caius confront one another threateningly, but the others manage to keep them apart. It soon becomes clear that the two men have been sent to different meeting points for the duel. The host cheerfully tells the gathering that it was his idea, as he did not want either man to suffer. To celebrate the fact that they are both unharmed, he suggests that they all retire to the inn for a drink:

| | |
|---|---|
| *Host:* | Shall I lose my doctor? No, he gives me the potions and the motions.[1] Shall I lose my parson? My priest? My Sir Hugh? No, he gives me the proverbs and the no-verbs[2] ... Boys of art,[3] I have deceived you both: I have directed you to wrong places. Your hearts are mighty, your skins are whole, and let burnt sack be the issue.[4] |

[1] *laxatives*
[2] *moral injunctions, prohibitions*
[3] *skill, learning*
[4] *let's bring the matter to an end with a glass of mulled wine*

As the others set off for the Garter, Caius and Sir Hugh remain behind. Both men feel deeply offended by the host's interference in their duel. Putting aside their own differences, they agree that they must avenge this insult to their honour:

> Evans:   I desire you that we may be friends, and let us knog
>          our prains together[1] to be revenge on this same scall,
>          scurvy, cogging companion,[2] the host of the Garter.
> Caius:   By gar, with all my heart. He promise to bring me
>          where is Anne Page; by gar, he deceive me too.
> Evans:   Well, I will smite his noddles.[3]
>
> [1] *put our heads together, confer*
> [2] *scabby, contemptible, lying rascal*
> [3] *thump his head*

---

In the late 1590s, many playwrights – partly as a reaction against the romantic, magical or historical settings of many earlier plays – were becoming interested in 'city comedies'. These were realistic plays with a satirical edge, usually set in London, with a cast of characters drawn from everyday city life.

The city comedy genre does not seem to have appealed greatly to Shakespeare. *The Merry Wives of Windsor* comes close, in that it is his only play set in contemporary England, but it retains a distinctive Shakespearean stamp:

*"Shakespeare never forgot that he was the grandson of a yeoman farmer and the son of a provincial shopkeeper ... Nor did he ever forget that he belonged to the country, not the city. His most English comedy,* The Merry Wives of Windsor, *is signally located not in London but in bourgeois small-town Windsor, a place far more like Stratford (albeit with a royal castle on its doorstep)."*

Jonathan Bate, *Soul of the Age*, 2009

---

# A dramatic revelation is planned

Mistress Page is on her way to see her friend Mistress Ford. Falstaff's young servant, Robin, is with her: he is to act as messenger between the knight and the two women.

When Master Ford comes across them, he is shocked to learn of the identity of the Page family's new servant:

*Ford:*  Where had you this pretty weathercock? [1]
*Mistress Page:*  I cannot tell what the dickens his name is my husband had him of. [2] – What do you call your knight's name, sirrah?
*Robin:*  Sir John Falstaff.
*Ford:*  Sir John Falstaff?

[1] *colourfully dressed little boy*
[2] *I can't remember who my husband got him from*

Mistress Page and the boy move on, leaving Ford horrified. Clearly Page's wife, just like his own, is conducting a secret affair with Falstaff. He is frustrated with Master Page; the man's complete lack of jealousy has made him oblivious to his wife's obvious infidelity.

Ford knows, from his disguised encounter with Falstaff, that the knight has a rendezvous with his wife this morning. He hears the clock strike, and realises that the two of them are together at this very moment. He heads for his house, determined to rush in unexpectedly and catch them off guard. His discovery will shake Page out of his complacency, and make everyone realise that his own supposed jealousy is entirely justified:

*Ford:*  [*clock strikes*] The clock gives me my cue, and my assurance bids me search: [1] there I shall find Falstaff. I shall be rather praised for this than mocked, for it is as positive as the earth is firm that Falstaff is there. I will go.

[1] *I am driven on by the certainty that I am correct*

The men involved in the abortive duel now come into view, on their way back from Frogmore: the two reconciled rivals, doctor Caius and Sir Hugh; Justice Shallow and Master Page, with Anne Page's hopeful suitor Slender; and the host of the Garter Inn. Ford invites them to his house, secretly pleased to have an audience for the revelation of his wife's illicit encounter with Falstaff.

Shallow declines the invitation; he is to dine with Anne Page, and hopes to persuade her to marry young Slender. Master Page mentions that he is in favour of the match, although his wife would prefer their daughter to marry the doctor. Caius is pleased to hear it, and points out that his housekeeper, Mistress Quickly, has already assured him that he is Anne's preferred choice of husband. There is a third candidate, the host mentions, who seems very promising:

*Host:* What say you to young Master Fenton? He capers,[1] he dances, he has eyes of youth, he writes verses, he speaks holiday,[2] he smells April and May:[3] he will carry't[4] ...

[1] *is merry and lively*
[2] *uses witty, entertaining language*
[3] *is as fresh as springtime*
[4] *succeed, win*

Page flatly refuses to countenance the idea. He believes that Fenton, despite his aristocratic connections, is disreputable and extravagant: if he marries Anne in the hope of getting at Page's money, he will be sorely disappointed.

Shallow and Slender now leave for their appointment with Anne Page, and the host returns to his inn. Ford repeats his invitation to the others, confident that a surprise awaits them, and they all set off for his house:

*Ford:* I beseech you heartily, some of you go home with me to dinner. Besides your cheer[1] you shall have sport: I will show you a monster.[2] Master Doctor, you shall go; so shall you, Master Page, and you, Sir Hugh.

[1] *food and drink*
[2] *a strange, hideous creature; Falstaff*

# A declaration of love

At Ford's house, meanwhile, Mistresses Page and Ford are preparing for the imminent arrival of Falstaff. They are confident that Mistress Ford's enthusiastic response to Sir John's love-letter, communicated through Mistress Quickly, has had the desired effect. The knight, aware that Master Ford is out of the house for a couple of hours, should arrive soon expecting a romantic assignation.

Two servants now bring in a large laundry basket. Mistress Ford reminds them of their instructions, which must be followed to the letter even though they may seem strange. On her command, they are to carry the basket away and dump its contents, without hesitation, into the filthy sludge at the river's edge:

> *Mistress Ford:* … when I suddenly call you, come forth and, without any pause or staggering, take this basket on your shoulders. That done, trudge with it in all haste, and carry it among the whitsters[1] in Datchet Mead, and there empty it in the muddy ditch close by the Thames side.

[1] *bleachers, professional cleaners of linen*

---

A best-selling book of Shakespeare's time provided a wealth of information on every conceivable aspect of running a household. Included among the recipes and domestic tips was detailed guidance on womanly conduct:

*"… our English housewife must be of chaste thought, stout courage, patient, untired, watchful, diligent, witty, pleasant, constant in friendship, full of good neighbourhood, wise in discourse (but not frequently therein), sharp and quick of speech, but not bitter or talkative, secret in her affairs, comfortable[1] in her counsels, and generally skilful in all the worthy knowledges which do belong to her vocation."*

[1] *comforting, compassionate*

Gervase Markham, *The English Huswife: Containing the Inward and Outward Virtues which Ought to Be in a Complete Woman*, 1615

Young Robin now runs in to report that Falstaff is at the back door, and has asked to see Mistress Ford. When pressed by Mistress Page, the boy promises that Falstaff does not know that she too is present in the house.

Mistress Ford tells the boy to invite Falstaff in. Mistress Page, as arranged, leaves the room. Her friend reminds her to listen carefully, and to come back in at the agreed moment. The fat knight will be punished for his impertinence, she declares:

*Mistress Ford:*  Mistress Page, remember you your cue.
*Mistress Page:*  I warrant thee: if I do not act it, hiss me.[1]
*Mistress Ford:*  Go to, then. We'll use this unwholesome humidity,[2] this watery pumpion;[3] we'll teach him to know turtles from jays.[4]

> [1] *if I don't play my part properly, heckle me like a bad actor*
> [2] *we'll treat this bag of noxious fluids as he deserves*
> [3] *pumpkin*
> [4] *turtle doves symbolised love and faithfulness; jays were seen as gaudy, chattering and fickle*

No sooner has Mistress Page hurried out than Falstaff makes his entrance. He addresses Mistress Ford in extravagant, passionate terms:

*Falstaff:*  Have I caught thee, my heavenly jewel? Why, now let me die, for I have lived long enough: this is the period[1] of my ambition. O this blessed hour!
*Mistress Ford:*  O sweet Sir John!

> [1] *end point, achievement*

Maintaining that he is incapable of lying or hiding his true feelings, Falstaff goes even further, claiming that he would marry Mistress Ford if the opportunity arose. She replies that she is not worthy to join the ranks of the aristocracy:

> *Falstaff:* Mistress Ford, I cannot cog, I cannot prate [1] ... I would [2] thy husband were dead. I'll speak it before the best lord: [3] I would make thee my lady.
> *Mistress Ford:* I your lady, Sir John? Alas, I should be a pitiful lady.

> [1] *I cannot flatter dishonestly or prattle meaninglessly*
> [2] *wish*
> [3] *I'm prepared to proclaim it in front of anyone*

On the contrary, insists Falstaff, she is eminently suited to life in the highest circles of society; she has simply been held back, so far, by fortune. He insists, once again, that he is a simple, plain-speaking man who is utterly in love with her:

> *Falstaff:* Come, I cannot cog and say thou art this and that, [1] like a many of these lisping hawthorn buds that come like women in men's apparel, [2] and smell like Bucklersbury [3] in simple time. [4] I cannot – but I love thee, none but thee; and thou deservest it.

> [1] *flatter you with exaggerated compliments*
> [2] *effeminate young courtiers with pretentious manners*
> [3] *London street renowned for its herbalists*
> [4] *midsummer, when fresh supplies of aromatic herbs ('simples') were delivered*

Mistress Ford pretends to be concerned that Sir John may in fact be in love with her friend, Mistress Page. He laughs off the idea:

> *Mistress Ford:* Do not betray me, sir; I fear you love Mistress Page.
> *Falstaff:* Thou mightst as well say I love to walk by the Counter-gate, [1] which is as hateful to me as the reek of a lime-kiln. [2]

> [1] *entrance to a debtor's prison in Southwark, notorious for its foul smell*
> [2] *smoke from a furnace*

# An unwelcome interruption

The women's plan now swings into action. First, Robin runs in and announces breathlessly that an unexpected visitor has arrived. Falstaff immediately takes cover, not wanting his pursuit of Mistress Ford to become common knowledge:

| | |
|---|---|
| *Robin:* | Mistress Ford, Mistress Ford, here's Mistress Page at the door, sweating, and blowing,[1] and looking wildly, and would needs speak with you presently. |
| *Falstaff:* | She shall not see me; I will ensconce me behind the arras.[2] |

*Mistress Ford:* Pray you do so; she's a very tattling woman.[3]

[1] *puffing, panting*
[2] *I'll hide behind the tapestry hanging on the wall*
[3] *a terrible gossip*

Right on cue, Mistress Page now comes in. As she had promised, she plays her part enthusiastically, and makes a dramatic announcement:

*Mistress Page:* O Mistress Ford, what have you done? You're shamed, you're overthrown, you're undone for ever!

Mistress Ford's jealous husband is on his way home, she warns: he is convinced that she is having a secret affair in his absence. A band of citizens and officials is with him, and they intend to search the house and find the guilty man. Mistress Page pretends to be shocked at the very idea, but her friend admits that her husband is right. Her clandestine visitor is in the house at this very moment:

*Mistress Page:* Pray heaven it be not so, that you have such a man here. But 'tis most certain your husband's coming, with half Windsor at his heels, to search for such a one …

*Mistress Ford:* What shall I do? There is a gentleman, my dear friend; and I fear not mine own shame so much as his peril. I had rather than a thousand pound he were out of the house.

Both women agree that the man in question must be removed from the house urgently. They pretend to notice the large, empty laundry basket all of a sudden: perhaps he could be carried out in it? Mistress Ford thinks it is too small:

> Mistress Page: ... bethink you of some conveyance [1] – in the house you cannot hide him. – O, how have you deceived me! Look, here is a basket: if he be of any reasonable stature, he may creep in here, and throw foul linen upon him, as if it were going to bucking [2] ...
>
> Mistress Ford: He's too big to go in there. What shall I do?

[1] *think of some way of getting him out*
[2] *we could cover him with dirty clothes, as if the basket were being taken to the laundry*

Falstaff, desperate to escape, ignores the concerns about his size, and jumps out from behind the tapestry. Mistress Page feigns surprise. Claiming to be outraged that he appears to be involved with Mistress Ford, she shows him the love-letters he sent her. Falstaff assures her that she, not Mistress Ford, is the one he truly loves:

> Mistress Page: What, Sir John Falstaff? [*aside, to Falstaff*] Are these your letters, knight?
>
> Falstaff: [*aside, to Mistress Page*] I love thee, and none but thee. Help me away. Let me creep in here ...

---

> "Thirty-six big plays in five blank verse acts, and not a single hero! Only one man in them all who believes in life, enjoys life, thinks life worth living ... and that man – Falstaff!"
>
> George Bernard Shaw, *Better than Shakespear?*, preface to *Three Plays for Puritans*, 1901

---

Falstaff squeezes himself into the laundry basket with difficulty, and the two women pile dirty linen on top of him. Mistress Ford then calls out for her two servants to carry the basket away: they have previously been instructed, whatever else may be said, to dump its contents into a muddy ditch.

## The intruder vanishes

Everything has gone according to plan. Mistresses Ford and Page have fooled Falstaff into thinking that the jealous Master Ford is on his way home, and as a result Sir John will be taken away and tipped unceremoniously into the mire at the edge of the Thames.

Unbeknown to the women, however, Ford really *is* approaching; in his disguise as Master Brook, he has learnt of his wife's invitation to Falstaff, and is determined to burst in on their amorous meeting. Just as the laundry basket is being carried out, Ford arrives, promising his sceptical companions that he will show them proof of his wife's infidelity. Mistress Ford, thinking quickly, teases her husband for his interest in the basket:

> *Ford:* [*to his companions*] Pray you, come near. If I suspect without cause, why, then make sport at me, then let me be your jest, I deserve it. [*to the servants carrying the laundry basket*] How now? Whither bear you this? [1]
>
> *Servant:* To the laundress,[2] forsooth.
>
> *Mistress Ford:* Why, what have you to do whither they bear it? You were best meddle with buck-washing![3]

> [1] *where are you carrying this basket?*
> [2] *washerwoman*
> [3] *you're hardly the right person to be bothered about the laundry*

The servants leave with the laundry basket. Ford now announces that the house will be searched. He produces his keys and, after locking the front door, invites his guests to come upstairs with him and search through all the rooms, closets and cupboards in the house.

Ford does not name the culprit, but promises that his wife's secret lover will be found. Master Page is uncomfortable with his friend's obsessive jealousy:

| | |
|---|---|
| *Ford:* | Gentleman, I have dreamed tonight;[1] I'll tell you my dream. Here, here, here be my keys: ascend my chambers, search, seek, find out. I'll warrant we'll unkennel the fox.[2] Let me stop this way first. [*locks the door*] So, now escape![3] |
| *Page:* | Good Master Ford, be contented; you wrong yourself too much.[4] |

[1] *last night*
[2] *force our prey out of his hiding place*
[3] *let's see if he can escape now*
[4] *restrain yourself; your attitude is harming you*

Ford heads upstairs, calling out to his companions to join him. Sir Hugh and doctor Caius, like Page, are troubled by Ford's excessive enthusiasm:

| | |
|---|---|
| *Ford:* | Up, gentlemen, you shall see sport anon.[1] Follow me, gentlemen. |
| *Evans:* | By Jeshu, this is fery fantastical humours and jealousies. |
| *Caius:* | By gar, 'tis no the fashion of France; it is not jealous[2] in France. |

[1] *you'll see something entertaining in a minute*
[2] *this would not be a cause for jealousy*

As the others go from room to room upstairs, the two women rejoice in their good luck. Falstaff's despatch to a muddy ditch has been made even more gratifying by the unexpected return of Master Ford, whose search will prove fruitless:

*Mistress Page:* Is there not a double excellency in this?
*Mistress Ford:* I know not which pleases me better, that my husband is deceived, or Sir John.

Mistress Ford, unaware that her husband had previously visited Falstaff in disguise, is concerned that he seems more than usually jealous; it is as if he knew in advance about Sir John's plan to visit her. In order to find out, Mistress Page believes that further trickery will be needed. Besides, Falstaff needs to learn his lesson:

> *Mistress Ford:* I think my husband hath some special suspicion of Falstaff's being here, for I never saw him so gross[1] in his jealousy till now.
>
> *Mistress Page:* I will lay a plot to try that,[2] and we will yet have more tricks with Falstaff. His dissolute disease will scarce obey this medicine.[3]
>
> > [1] *extreme, blatant*
> > [2] *to find out if that is true*
> > [3] *the treatment we have given him today will hardly be enough to cure his debauchery*

The women decide to send Mistress Quickly to visit Falstaff again, with instructions to apologise on their behalf and ask him for another meeting tomorrow morning. The fat knight will be unable to resist, and with luck they will be able to give him his just deserts for a second time.

Master Ford now comes downstairs with his companions. He is crestfallen, having failed to produce the dramatic revelation he had hoped for. An offhand comment gives away the fact that Ford has, as the women suspected, been in touch with Falstaff:

> *Ford:* I cannot find him. Maybe the knave bragged of that he could not compass.[1]
>
> *Mistress Page:* [*aside, to Mistress Ford* ] Heard you that?
>
> > [1] *boasted of something he couldn't achieve in reality*

Ford's companions are unanimous in their criticism: clearly his wife is honest, and he is dreadfully misguided in his jealousy. He claims, in response, that it is a flaw in his character that he cannot control:

| | |
|---|---|
| *Page:* | Fie, fie, Master Ford, are you not ashamed? What spirit, what devil, suggests this imagination? [1] I would not ha' your distemper in this kind [2] for the wealth of Windsor Castle. |
| *Ford:* | 'Tis my fault, [3] Master Page, I suffer for it. |

[1] *causes these delusions*
[2] *mental disturbance of this sort*
[3] *weakness, misfortune*

Apologising profusely, Ford asks his guests to stay at his house for a meal. Page mentions that he intends to go hunting the next morning, and invites his friends to take part. Ford, Caius and Sir Hugh all agree to join him.

Before they join the others for the meal, Sir Hugh and Caius have a brief discussion. They have not forgotten their humiliation at the hands of the host of the Garter, who made a mockery of their duel by sending them to different meeting-places. Tomorrow, they agree, they will take their revenge.

Charles Dickens – who referred to Shakespeare as 'the great master' – was an enthusiastic participant in amateur dramatics. In 1848 he and a group of friends presented *The Merry Wives of Windsor* at the Theatre Royal in London, with profits going towards the upkeep of Shakespeare's birthplace in Stratford-upon-Avon. (Dickens had earlier been involved in the purchase of the house for the nation, preventing it from going into private hands.)

Dickens, although only thirty-six, played the part of Justice Shallow. A fellow performer was greatly impressed by his acting talent:

*"His impersonation was perfect: the old, stiff limbs, the senile stoop of the shoulders, the head bent with age, the feeble step, with a certain attempted smartness of carriage characteristic of the conceited Justice of the Peace, were all assumed and maintained with wonderful accuracy."*

Mary Cowden Clarke, *Recollections of Writers*, 1878

# Fenton is determined

Outside Page's house, Fenton is talking to Anne, complaining that her father's disapproval may make it impossible for them to marry. He realises that Master Page thinks of him as an impoverished, dissolute aristocrat, interested in Anne only for her money. She challenges him, suggesting that her father may be right. Fenton denies the charge passionately; he admits that her family's wealth aroused his interest at first, but his love for her is now absolutely sincere. Anne urges him to try again to win her father's blessing:

> *Fenton:*　　　　　　… I will confess thy father's wealth
> 　　　　　Was the first motive that I wooed thee, Anne,
> 　　　　　Yet, wooing thee, I found thee of more value
> 　　　　　Than stamps[1] in gold or sums in sealed bags;
> 　　　　　And 'tis the very riches of thyself
> 　　　　　That now I aim at.
> *Anne:*　　　　　　　　Gentle Master Fenton,
> 　　　　　Yet seek[2] my father's love, still seek it, sir …
>
> [1] *coins, stamped with the monarch's head*
> [2] *keep trying to gain*

The lovers' conversation is interrupted by the arrival of Slender and his elderly relative Shallow. With them is Mistress Quickly, who has promised to help with their quest to match Slender with Anne Page.

Mistress Quickly takes Fenton to one side, and urges Anne to talk to Slender. The girl approaches reluctantly, considering the young man repulsive even though he is her father's choice as her future husband. Slender is an inept conversationalist, and Shallow attempts to speak for him:

> *Slender:*　Pray you, uncle, tell Mistress Anne the jest of how my
> 　　　　father stole two geese out of a pen, good uncle.
> *Shallow:*　Mistress Anne, my cousin loves you.
> *Slender:*　Ay, that I do, as well as I love any woman in
> 　　　　Gloucestershire.
> *Shallow:*　He will maintain you like a gentlewoman.

Anne asks Slender to speak for himself, and it quickly becomes clear that the slow-witted youth has no deep feelings for her:

| | |
|---|---|
| *Anne:* | Now, Master Slender. |
| *Slender:* | Now, good Mistress Anne. |
| *Anne:* | What is your will? [1] |
| *Slender:* | My will? 'Od's heartlings,[2] that's a pretty jest indeed! I ne'er made my will yet, I thank God: I am not such a sickly creature, I give God praise. |
| *Anne:* | I mean, Master Slender, what would you with me? |
| *Slender:* | Truly, for mine own part, I would little or nothing with you. Your father and my uncle hath made motions [3] ... |

[1] *what do you want?*
[2] *by God's heart*
[3] *proposed the idea that I should marry you*

Master Page and his wife now appear. Page is pleased to see Slender, and urges his daughter to treat him lovingly. He is irritated, however, when he notices that Fenton is present, and orders the young man to stay away from his daughter.

Page warmly invites Shallow and Slender into his house. As the men leave, Fenton appeals to Mistress Page, and Anne adds her voice to his appeal. She is dismayed to hear that her mother has another suitor in mind, the volatile doctor Caius. She finds him equally abhorrent:

| | |
|---|---|
| *Fenton:* | ... against all checks, rebukes and manners,[1] I must advance the colours of my love And not retire.[2] Let me have your good will. |
| *Anne:* | Good mother, do not marry me to yond fool.[3] |
| *Mistress Page:* | I mean it not, I seek you a better husband. |
| *Mistress Quickly:* | [*aside, to Anne*] That's my master, Master Doctor. |
| *Anne:* | Alas, I had rather be set quick [4] i'th' earth, And bowled to death with turnips! |

[1] *in spite of all obstacles and criticism, and disregarding normal good manners*
[2] *raise the flag in my campaign to marry Anne, and not give up*
[3] *Slender*
[4] *alive*

Mistress Page promises Fenton that she will not ignore her daughter's feelings:

> *Mistress Page:*                … good Master Fenton,
> I will not be your friend, nor enemy.
> My daughter will I question how she loves you,
> And as I find her, so am I affected.[1]
>
> [1] *whatever she says will influence me*

Anne and her mother go indoors. Mistress Quickly, alone with Fenton, boasts that she is the one who has persuaded Mistress Page to look favourably on him:

> *Mistress Quickly:* This is my doing, now. 'Nay,' said I, 'will you cast away your child on a fool, and a physician? Look on Master Fenton!' This is my doing.

Fenton hands her some money as a reward. When he leaves, Mistress Quickly reflects that she has no particular preference among the three suitors. Indeed, she has acted as a go-between for all of them:

> *Mistress Quickly:* A kind heart he hath: a woman would run through fire and water for such a kind heart. But yet I would my master[1] had Mistress Anne, or I would Master Slender had her; or, in sooth,[2] I would Master Fenton had her. I will do what I can for them all three, for so I have promised, and I'll be as good as my word …
>
> [1] *Caius*
> [2] *truthfully, honestly*

At this point, Mistress Quickly suddenly remembers she has another errand. Mistresses Page and Ford have asked her to speak to Falstaff; she is to apologise for his earlier treatment, and ask him to visit Mistress Ford again tomorrow morning.

In 1720, the manager of the Lincoln's Inn Fields Theatre in London decided to produce a revival of *The Merry Wives of Windsor*, a play which had not been staged in its original form for many years. Finding it difficult to identify a suitable Falstaff, he reluctantly agreed to offer the part to one of his younger actors, the 27-year-old James Quin.

The production was a great success, and the play once more became a regular fixture on the London stage. Quin, in particular, was hugely popular as Falstaff, and played the role over 150 times during his long career. He acted at several London theatres, spending the last fifteen years of his career at Covent Garden. In 1750, another theatre tried to tempt the 57-year-old actor away: Quin responded by demanding – and receiving – a salary of £1,000 a year to remain at Covent Garden, the highest amount paid to any actor at the time.

# A second chance                                                    III, v

It is early morning, and in his room at the Garter Inn Falstaff is feeling sorry for himself. He is still recovering from being dumped in the muddy Thames after his escape from Ford's house yesterday, and he calls for a tankard of his usual wine.

Falstaff consoles himself with the thought that the water into which he was tipped was not too deep. He has a horror of drowning, and imagines the scene if he had not managed to climb out:

> *Falstaff:*  … you may know by my size that I have a kind of alacrity in sinking:[1] if the bottom were as deep as hell, I should down.[2] I had been drowned, but that the shore was shelvy and shallow – a death that I abhor, for the water swells a man – and what a thing should I have been, when I had been swelled? I should have been a mountain of mummy![3]
>
> [1] *my body sinks rapidly and unstoppably*
> [2] *descend, keep on sinking*
> [3] *dead flesh*

Falstaff's companion Bardolph, now a servingman at the Garter, arrives with his drink, and announces that Mistress Quickly is at the door. She comes in, and when Falstaff hears who has sent her, his reply is abrupt and hostile:

*Mistress Quickly:* Marry, sir, I come to your worship from Mistress Ford.
*Falstaff:* Mistress Ford? I have had ford [1] enough. I was thrown into the ford, I have my belly full of ford.

[1] *river water*

Mistress Ford is mortified at Sir John's ill-treatment, the messenger reports; it was the result of a misunderstanding by her servants. Falstaff's mood changes instantly when he hears that Master Ford will be out hunting later this morning. The lady, apparently, is eager for another visit in his absence. Falstaff accepts, while insisting that he must be treated with care this time:

*Mistress Quickly:* Well, she laments, sir, for it, that it would yearn your heart [1] to see it. Her husband goes this morning a-birding. [2] She desires you once more to come to her, between eight and nine. I must carry her word [3] quickly; she'll make you amends, I warrant you.
*Falstaff:* Well, I will visit her; tell her so, and bid her think what a man is. Let her consider his frailty ...

[1] *so much that it would move you to feel pity*
[2] *hunting birds*
[3] *take a message back to her*

Mistress Quickly leaves on her errand. Falstaff remarks that Master Brook, the wealthy individual who hopes to seduce Mistress Ford, has not yet returned as promised. At this moment, Brook himself – in reality Master Ford in disguise – arrives, and immediately asks the knight about his visit to Mistress Ford.

Falstaff gives a vivid, embellished account of their unsuccessful meeting. The lady was delighted to see him, he explains, but her jealous husband returned at the crucial moment:

*Ford:* Did she change her determination? [1]
*Falstaff:* No, Master Brook, but the peaking cornuto [2] her

husband, Master Brook, dwelling in a continual 'larum of jealousy,[3] comes me in the instant of our encounter, after we had embraced, kissed, protested,[4] and, as it were, spoke the prologue of our comedy ...

[1] *decision, intention*
[2] *mean-spirited cuckold*
[3] *who lives in a constant state of fearful jealousy*
[4] *declared our love for one another*

Ford and his companions searched the house, Falstaff reports, but he escaped thanks to Mistress Page. Under his disguise, Ford is stunned as he realises how close he had been to discovering the intruder in his house:

*Ford:*  And did he search for you, and could not find you?
*Falstaff:* You shall hear. As good luck would have it, comes in one Mistress Page, gives intelligence of Ford's approach; and in her invention, and Ford's wife's distraction,[1] they conveyed me into a buck-basket.[2]
*Ford:*  A buck-basket?

[1] *Mistress Page had the idea, and Mistress Ford distracted her husband's attention*
[2] *laundry basket*

Falstaff is determined that Brook should know how much trouble he has been through; after all, the eventual aim is that Falstaff's seduction of Mistress Ford should enable Brook to do the same. He describes in lurid detail how he was crammed into the basket, had dirty clothes piled on top of him, became excruciatingly hot and uncomfortable, and finally ended up in the river:

*Falstaff:* ... it was a miracle to scape suffocation. And in the height of this bath[1] – when I was more than half stewed in grease, like a Dutch dish – to be thrown into the Thames and cooled, glowing hot, in that surge like a horseshoe[2] – think of that – hissing hot – think of that, Master Brook.

[1] *soaking in sweat*
[2] *like a red-hot horseshoe plunged into water by the blacksmith to cool*

Brook apologises, and suggests that the plan to seduce Mistress Ford will have to be abandoned. Falstaff contradicts him at once: indeed, a meeting is planned this very morning. He has learnt from his informant that Ford is due to go out hunting today, and Mistress Ford has again invited him to take advantage of her husband's absence:

Ford:     My suit, then, is desperate:[1] you'll undertake[2] her no more?

Falstaff:  Master Brook, I will be thrown into Etna, as I have been into Thames, ere I will leave her thus. Her husband is this morning gone a-birding; I have received from her another embassy[3] of meeting ...

[1] *my quest is hopeless*
[2] *approach, attempt to win*
[3] *message, request*

Falstaff suddenly realises that it is time to leave for his appointment with Mistress Ford. As he hurries away, he reassures Brook that he will succeed with the lady this time.

---

*"Falstaff is repeatedly humiliated, but his mastery of the English language always gives him the last word ... By redescribing farcical action in words of mock-epic excess, verbally re-enacting the ducking from the point of view of the ducked, Falstaff embodies his creator's greatest achievement: the triumph of the English language."*

Jonathan Bate, Introduction to the RSC edition of *The Merry Wives of Windsor*, 2011

Left alone, Ford rouses himself to action. Rather than meekly accept his wife's infidelity, he resolves to catch Falstaff and expose the illicit lovers. He will search the house from top to bottom, and will not make the same mistake again:

Ford: Is this a vision? Is this a dream? Do I sleep? Master Ford, awake; awake, Master Ford! ... I will now take the lecher. He is at my house, he cannot scape me – 'tis impossible he should. He cannot creep into a half-penny purse, nor into a pepperbox. But, lest the devil that guides him should aid him,[1] I will search impossible places.

[1] *in case the devil helps him to squeeze into a tiny space*

## A reluctant student IV, i

Mistress Page is taking her young son, William, to school. She is talking to Mistress Quickly about Falstaff: following his invitation earlier today, Sir John should be at Mistress Ford's by now. Mistress Page intends to visit her friend shortly, so that the two of them can continue with their punishment of the lecherous knight.

William's teacher, Sir Hugh, now appears: he informs them that a holiday has been declared, so there is no school today for the boy. Mistress Page mentions that her son is making poor progress in his Latin, and asks Sir Hugh to give him an impromptu test. The combination of the parson's thick accent and his confused approach to teaching makes proceedings difficult:

Evans: What is *lapis*, William?
William: A stone.
Evans: And what is 'a stone', William?
William: A pebble.
Evans: No, it is *lapis*; I pray you, remember in your prain.[1]

[1] *brain*

Mistress Quickly listens intently, despite knowing no Latin, and interrupts repeatedly. Hearing various Latin forms of 'this' and 'these' – *hic, haec, hoc, horum* and *harum* – she decides that the parson's teaching is immoral, and she scolds him for introducing William to disreputable habits at his young age:

> *Mistress Quickly:* You do ill to teach the child such words. – He teaches him to hick[1] and to hack,[2] which they'll do fast enough of themselves, and to call 'whore 'em'![3] – Fie upon you!
>
> *Evans:* 'Oman, art thou lunatics? Hast thou no understandings for thy cases, and the numbers of the genders?

[1] *to hiccup, from drinking too much*
[2] *to keep company with prostitutes*
[3] *treat them like whores*

Mistress Page, becoming impatient, sends the boy back home and hurries away to join Mistress Ford.

## Thwarted again

IV, ii

Falstaff has come to see Mistress Ford, unable to resist her invitation despite his earlier experience. She has apologised profusely for his mistreatment, and he accepts her apologies with an elaborate show of graciousness. She will find him to be the perfect courtly lover, he promises:

> *Falstaff:* Mistress Ford, your sorrow hath eaten up my sufferance.[1] I see you are obsequious[2] in your love and I profess requital to a hair's breadth,[3] not only, Mistress Ford, in the simple office of love, but in all the accoutrement, compliment and ceremony of it.[4]

[1] *has made up for my suffering*
[2] *dutiful, obedient*
[3] *I undertake to return your love in full*
[4] *both as a lover and in all the formalities, language and etiquette of love*

Falstaff is anxious to establish that Mistress Ford's husband will not return imminently, and she confirms that he is out hunting with his friends. However, at this very moment a voice is heard at the door: it is Mistress Page, who has an urgent message for her friend. Just as she enters, Mistress Ford hastily ushers Falstaff into a nearby hiding-place.

The two women now hold a carefully planned conversation, speaking loudly to ensure that Falstaff can hear. Mistress Page first asks whether there is anyone else in the house, and Mistress Ford claims that they are alone. That is just as well, replies Mistress Page; her husband is, once again, on his way home in a jealous rage, bringing his companions with him. He is convinced that Sir John is with his wife, and is determined to take revenge:

*Mistress Page:*  Why, woman, your husband is in his old lines [1]
again … any madness I ever yet beheld seemed but
tameness, civility and patience to this his distemper [2]
he is in now. I am glad the fat knight is not here.
*Mistress Ford:*  Why, does he talk of him?
*Mistress Page:*  Of none but him …

[1] *playing his old role*
[2] *compared to the tempestuous mood he is in now*

It is a good thing that Master Ford is coming home unexpectedly, Mistress Page tells her friend: since Falstaff is not present, her husband will finally realise that his suspicions are unfounded. Mistress Ford now makes a dramatic confession:

*Mistress Ford:*  How near is he, Mistress Page?
*Mistress Page:*  Hard by,[1] at street end. He will be here anon.[2]
*Mistress Ford:*  I am undone: the knight is here.
*Mistress Page:*  Why, then you are utterly shamed, and he's but [3]
a dead man. What a woman are you! Away with him,
away with him: better shame than murder.

[1] *very close*
[2] *any minute, shortly*
[3] *virtually, as good as*

Mistress Ford, putting on an act of frantic anxiety, mentions the laundry basket again, and at this point Falstaff comes out of his hiding place in a state of panic. He suggests running away before Ford returns, but Mistress Page's response leaves him even more terrified:

*Falstaff:* No, I'll come no more i'the basket. May I not go out ere he come? [1]

*Mistress Page:* Alas, three of Master Ford's brothers watch the door with pistols ...

[1] *before Ford returns*

Nowhere in the house will provide a safe refuge, says Mistress Ford: her husband will search every inch of the building, including cupboards, closets, wells and attics. It occurs to the women that he might escape in disguise. Falstaff, in desperation, begs them to think of something, and Mistress Ford suddenly remembers that there is a suitable frock in the house:

*Falstaff:* Good hearts, devise something; any extremity rather than a mischief.[1]

*Mistress Ford:* My maid's aunt, the fat woman of Brentford, has a gown above.[2]

*Mistress Page:* On my word, it will serve him. She's as big as he is ...

[1] *anything to avoid physical injury*
[2] *upstairs*

The women send Sir John upstairs to find the gown. They are delighted that everything is going according to plan. Mistress Ford's husband has a particular loathing for the lady in question, and Falstaff, despite his disguise, is unlikely to escape unscathed:

*Mistress Ford:* I would[1] my husband would meet him in this shape![2] He cannot abide the old woman of Brentford; he swears she's a witch, forbade her my house and has threatened to beat her.

[1] *wish, hope*
[2] *form, disguise*

Mistress Page confirms that her friend's husband is genuinely on his way home. He seems to have discovered, somehow, that Falstaff was previously smuggled out in the laundry basket. They decide to have the basket carried out again, in front of Master Ford, to see his reaction. In the meantime, they must help Falstaff to disguise himself as the infamous old woman of Brentford.

Giving Falstaff his just deserts is proving hugely enjoyable for the two women, but they feel that their antics are perfectly justified, and involve nothing malicious or shameful:

> *Mistress Ford:* We'll leave a proof, by that which we will do,
> Wives may be merry and yet honest too.

Master Ford is approaching. Mistress Ford instructs John and Robert, the two servants, to pick up the laundry basket as before. As she goes upstairs to help get Falstaff into his gown, the two men approach the basket uneasily:

> *John:* Come, come, take it up.
> *Robert:* Pray heaven it be not full of knight again.
> *John:* I hope not, I had as lief bear[1] so much lead.

> [1] *I would just as soon carry*

---

*The Merry Wives of Windsor* is the only play by Shakespeare which is named solely after its leading female characters:

*"Mistress Ford and Mistress Page are the driving brains behind the play, they are the cleverest people in the play and together they are more than the sum of their parts. What's brilliant is that the two of them together are an unstoppable force. They combat with Falstaff for our affection, but in terms of the mechanism of the play and the plot and intelligence within the play they absolutely come out on top."*

Director Rachel Kavanaugh, commenting on her 2002 Royal Shakespeare Company production of *The Merry Wives of Windsor*

# A witch is exorcised

Ford now rushes in purposefully with his unwilling companions. Master Page, Shallow, Caius and Sir Hugh are all convinced that Ford is deluded, but he insists that his wife's lover is hiding somewhere in the house.

Catching sight of his servants carrying the large laundry basket towards the door, Ford orders them to stop, convinced that he has found the culprit. He then calls for his wife to come downstairs. Perhaps she should inspect the contents of the basket, he remarks sarcastically:

Ford:      Set down the basket, villains … wife, I say! Come, come forth: behold what honest clothes you send forth to bleaching!

Page:      Why, this passes,[1] Master Ford! You are not to go loose any longer, you must be pinioned.[2]

[1] *is too much, is beyond belief*
[2] *be restrained; have your wings clipped, like a captive bird*

Mistress Ford comes downstairs. Onlookers should not be taken in by her apparent modesty and virtue, Master Ford declares dramatically. He opens the basket, certain that Falstaff is hiding inside, and starts to pull the dirty clothes out with grim determination. Ignoring his wife's protestations, he calls on his companions to help.

Soon the floor is covered with dirty linen, and the basket is empty. For a moment Ford is dejected; then, raising his spirits, he calls on his friends to help him search the house again. He is confident that he will be proved right:

Page:      Here's no man.

Shallow:  By my fidelity, this is not well, Master Ford, this wrongs[1] you.

Evans:    Master Ford, you must pray, and not follow the imaginations of your own heart: this is jealousies.

Ford:      Well, he's not here I seek for.

Page:      No, nor nowhere else but in your brain.

| Ford: | Help to search my house this one time. If I find not what I seek, show no colour for my extremity,[2] let me for ever be your table-sport.[3] |
|---|---|

[1] *shames, discredits*
[2] *if I fail to show a good reason for my extreme behaviour*
[3] *let me be a standing joke at social gatherings*

Mistress Ford now calls upstairs to Mistress Page, telling her to come down and bring the old woman with her. Ford is suspicious, and demands to know who they are talking about.

When it emerges that the woman in question is their maid's aunt, the old woman of Brentford, Ford is furious. She has a reputation for telling fortunes, and Ford is convinced that she deals with dark, supernatural powers. He believes her to be a witch, and has forbidden her from setting foot in his house. Ford grabs a cudgel impetuously and orders the woman to come downstairs:

| Ford: | We are simple men, we do not know what's brought to pass under the profession of fortune-telling.[1] She works by charms, by spells, by the figure,[2] and such daubery[3] as this is, beyond our element: we know nothing. – Come down, you witch, you hag, you! Come down, I say! |
|---|---|

[1] *what she may have caused to happen in the name of fortune-telling*
[2] *astrological signs*
[3] *trickery*

Mistress Page now appears. She treads slowly and carefully, as she is helping someone down the stairs. The figure appears to be a very large old lady, wrapped in a voluminous gown, bonnet and scarf; Falstaff has been successfully disguised.

Enraged to be confronted with the old woman of Brentford, Ford launches himself at her, hurling a stream of insults. He pounds her mercilessly with his cudgel as he orders her out of his home:

Ford:     Out of my door, you witch, you rag, you baggage, you polecat, you runnion,[1] out, out! I'll conjure you, I'll fortune-tell you![2]

[1] wretch, whore, old hag
[2] I'll teach you to cast spells and tell fortunes

An old tradition, dating back over three hundred years, maintains that *The Merry Wives of Windsor* was written in response to a request from Elizabeth I: the Queen was so taken with the character of Falstaff in the *Henry IV* plays that she immediately demanded another play featuring the corpulent knight, and showing him in love. The resulting comedy, according to this tradition, was written in two weeks, and had an enthusiastic reception from the Queen.

Very few scholars now believe the story to be completely accurate, but it can certainly be argued that the play was written hastily; in particular, it is almost entirely in prose, with only a tenth in verse. Most critics feel that the character of Falstaff, too, is portrayed more superficially here than in the *Henry IV* plays. Despite the undoubted popularity of *Merry Wives*, then, the play has its detractors. It has been suggested that Shakespeare wrote it hurriedly, even unwillingly, as a lucrative commission from a wealthy patron:

*"There are hints throughout that Shakespeare is uncomfortable with what he is doing and wishes to get it over with as rapidly as possible ... You can cram any fat man into a basket and get a laugh. He does not have to be Falstaff, nor need his creator be Shakespeare. By the time that Falstaff, disguised as a plump old woman, has absorbed a particularly nasty beating, one begins to conclude that Shakespeare loathes not only the occasion but himself for having yielded to it ... Commerce is commerce, but why did Shakespeare inflict this upon a character who represents his own wit at its most triumphant?"*

Harold Bloom, *Shakespeare: The Invention of the Human*, 1999

Once he has chased the evil old woman away, Ford turns to his friends. This time, he promises, he is certain that his wife's lover is hiding somewhere in the house: he wants them to witness the discovery of the intruder. They reluctantly agree, and head upstairs to help with the search:

*Ford:*    I beseech you, follow, see but the issue of my jealousy.[1] If I cry out thus upon no trail, never trust me when I open again.[2]

*Page:*    Let's obey his humour[3] a little further. Come, gentlemen.

> [1] the end result of acting on my suspicions
> [2] if I'm getting agitated about nothing, like an unreliable hunting dog, never take any notice of me in the future if I cause a disturbance
> [3] play along with his delusion

Mistresses Ford and Page, left alone downstairs, are overjoyed at the success of their second scheme to punish Falstaff. Perhaps he has learnt his lesson by now, they feel; either way, it is time to reveal to their husbands how and why they have dealt with Sir John. This should help, at least, to reduce Master Ford's excessive jealousy.

If any further punishment is decided on, declares Mistress Page, the two of them are the best people to hand it out:

*Mistress Ford:*  Shall we tell our husbands how we have served him?[1]

*Mistress Page:*  Yes, by all means, if it be but to scrape the figures[2] out of your husband's brains. If they can find in their hearts the poor unvirtuous fat knight shall be any further afflicted,[3] we two will still be the ministers.[4]

> [1] how we have treated Falstaff
> [2] just to erase the jealous imaginings
> [3] should be made to suffer any further
> [4] we will, again, be the ones to carry it out

In all likelihood, Masters Ford and Page will want to see the knight humiliated in public for his plot to seduce their wives and obtain their money. Mistress Page tells her friend that the two of them need to put their heads together straight away and come up with a scheme for a dramatic public revelation.

# Difficult customers

Back at the Garter Inn, the host is in a resentful mood. A group of German noblemen, claiming to be associates of an important Duke, have asked him to keep some rooms free. As a result, he has had to turn away other customers.

The host's assistant Bardolph now informs him that the Germans have requested some horses as they will shortly need to travel to court. They can have them, decides the host, but the cost will be extortionate:

> *Host:* They shall have my horses, but I'll make them pay,
> I'll sauce them.[1] They have had my house a week at
> command.[2] I have turned away my other guests: they
> must come off,[3] I'll sauce them.

> [1] *make them pay a high price*
> [2] *booked, at their disposal*
> [3] *pay up*

# The citizens unite

The truth about Falstaff has emerged at last. Ford and Page have read the identical love-letters that Falstaff sent to their wives, and have been told about his attempts at seduction. Page looks at the two letters with incredulity, while Ford is overcome with remorse:

> *Page:* And did he send you both these letters at an instant? [1]
> *Mistress Page:* Within a quarter of an hour.
> *Ford:* Pardon me, wife. Henceforth do what thou wilt: [2]
> I rather will suspect the sun with cold
> Than thee with wantonness.[3]

> [1] *at the same time*
> [2] *whatever you want*
> [3] *debauchery, unfaithfulness*

Page quickly becomes impatient with his friend's apologetic tone: his expressions of regret are almost as extravagant as his earlier jealous outbursts. The important thing is to expose Falstaff's deceitfulness to public scrutiny:

| Ford: | [*to Mistress Ford*] Now doth thy honour stand, |
| | In him that was of late an heretic,[1] |
| | As firm as faith. |
| Page: | 'Tis well, 'tis well, no more. |
| | Be not as extreme in submission as in offence.[2] |
| | But let our plot go forward. Let our wives |
| | Yet once again, to make us public sport,[3] |
| | Appoint a meeting with this old fat fellow, |
| | Where we may take him and disgrace him for it. |

[1] *misguided, an unbeliever*
[2] *don't be as extreme in your apology as you were in
    the fault for which you're apologising*
[3] *to entertain us all*

The two wives have come up with a plan that involves a rendezvous at midnight in Windsor Park. Master Page and Sir Hugh are doubtful, believing that Falstaff will not run the risk of further misfortunes. Mistress Ford is confident, however, that the fat knight can be tempted to another meeting.

Mistress Page introduces their plan by describing the legend of Herne the Hunter, the spirit of a dead forest warden who is seen on winter nights in the vicinity of an ancient oak tree. This ghostly figure, with fearsome antlers on his head, is said to strike terror into local inhabitants:

| Mistress Page: | There is an old tale goes that Herne the Hunter, |
| | Sometime[1] a keeper here in Windsor Forest, |
| | Doth, all the winter time, at still midnight, |
| | Walk round about an oak, with great ragg'd[2] horns, |
| | And there he blasts the trees, and takes the cattle,[3] |
| | And makes milch-kine yield blood,[4] and shakes a chain |
| | In a most hideous and dreadful manner. |

[1] *previously, once*
[2] *jagged, rough*
[3] *makes the trees wither and casts a spell on the cattle*
[4] *makes the dairy cows produce blood instead of milk*

The legend was widely believed in the past, says Mistress Page; even now, her husband confirms, there are plenty of superstitious people who are afraid to approach Herne's oak at night.

Herne – so the legend goes – was the King's head forester at Windsor. He maintained and protected the forest, which was the King's favourite hunting-ground, ensuring that there were plentiful populations of deer and wild boar.

Herne's companions, jealous of his success, conspired to kill him. One night a shady figure approached them, offering to do the deed himself in return for payment. There was a terrible thunderstorm that night; and in the morning, Herne was found dead at the foot of a great oak tree.

Soon things started to go wrong in the forest. Deer died or went missing for no apparent reason, and there were rumours of a ghostly hunter roaming the area. One night, when the conspirators had gathered once more, the shady figure who had offered to help them returned. It was none other than the Devil himself: and he wanted payment.

The next morning, the conspirators were found hanging from the great oak tree. Their tormented spirits, it is said, can still be seen on winter nights as they ride through the forest on their never-ending hunt; and at their head is the terrible horned figure of Herne the Hunter.

Mistress Ford goes on to explain that they will ask Falstaff to come to the infamous oak tree at midnight, in the guise of Herne himself, complete with horns and a chain. The two women will be waiting for him: but as soon as Falstaff arrives, a band of children disguised as fairies will surround him, and the women will run off.

The fairies, chanting noisily, will torment him by pinching him and singeing him with their candles, and will demand that he tell the truth about his misdeeds. At this point the citizens of Windsor will appear:

*Mistress Page:*     The truth being known,
        We'll all present ourselves, dishorn the spirit,[1]
        And mock him home to Windsor.

[1] *remove the antlers from the disguised Falstaff*

The idea is received enthusiastically. Parson Evans volunteers to teach the children their roles, while Master Page proposes to buy masks and material for their fairy costumes. Master Ford, for his part, will disguise himself as Brook again and make sure that the knight intends to accept his invitation to the midnight meeting.

The fate of Falstaff, however, is not the only subject on the Pages' minds. Master Page reveals, in an aside, that the planned encounter will provide an opportunity for his daughter and Slender to slip away and get married:

> *Mistress Page:* My Nan[1] shall be the queen of all the fairies,
> Finely attired in a robe of white.
> *Page:* That silk will I go buy – [*aside*] and in that time
> Shall Master Slender steal my Nan away,
> And marry her at Eton.

> [1] *Anne*

Mistress Page, too, has decided that it is time to act in the matter of her daughter's marriage. She has a different suitor in mind, the wealthy and well connected doctor Caius:

> *Mistress Page:* [*aside*] I'll to the Doctor: he hath my good will,
> And none but he, to marry with Nan Page.
> That Slender, though well landed,[1] is an idiot –
> And he my husband best of all affects.[2]
> The Doctor is well moneyed, and his friends
> Potent at court: he, none but he, shall have her ...

> [1] *in possession of a good amount of land*
> [2] *likes, favours*

## The wise woman speaks IV, v

Slender's servant Simple has come to the Garter. A stout old woman, thought to be the famous fortune-teller from Brentford, has been seen heading towards Falstaff's lodgings, and Simple hopes to talk to her. The host, concerned that a stranger may have broken in, calls out for Falstaff. The fat knight himself comes down; the old woman of Brentford was with him a moment ago, he confirms, but she has now left.

Simple is disappointed, as his master wanted to consult the woman on some important matters. The first concerns the theft of a valuable item from Slender. Luckily, says Falstaff, he talked to the wise woman about this very subject, and she stated that the article was stolen by a thief, an answer that appears to satisfy Simple.

The visitor is reluctant to mention the other matter his master wishes to discuss, as it is more personal. Falstaff demands to hear about it, and again it emerges that the old woman of Brentford has already made a pronouncement on the question:

*Simple:*    I would[1] I could have spoken with the woman herself. I had other things to have spoken with her too, from him.[2]
*Falstaff:*   What are they? Let us know.
*Host:*      Ay, come. Quick!
*Simple:*    I may not conceal[3] them, sir.
*Host:*      Conceal them, or thou diest.
*Simple:*    Why, sir, they were nothing but about Mistress Anne Page, to know if it were my master's fortune to have her, or no.
*Falstaff:*   'Tis, 'tis his fortune.
*Simple:*    What, sir?
*Falstaff:*   To have her, or no. Go, say the woman told me so.

[1] *wish*
[2] *as instructed by my master Slender*
[3] *reveal*

Delighted with the wise woman's verdict, Simple runs off to report the good news to his master. The host congratulates Falstaff on his answers, and asks sceptically whether the old woman of Brentford really was in his room. Falstaff, reflecting on the painful lesson he was given while in disguise, assures him that he is telling the truth:

*Host:*      Thou art clerkly,[1] thou art clerkly, Sir John. Was there a wise woman with thee?
*Falstaff:*   Ay, that there was, mine host; one that hath taught me more wit than ever I learnt before in my life; and I paid nothing for it neither, but was paid for my learning.[2]

[1] *learned, scholarly*
[2] *was paid (with a beating) for the lesson I received*

# A criminal gang at large

At this point Bardolph rushes in, covered in mud, in a state of alarm. The three Germans who asked to borrow the host's horses, claiming to be on their way to court to accompany a famous Duke, have turned out to be impostors. While accompanying the group, Bardolph has just been pushed out of the saddle. The three of them then raced away:

*Host:* Where be my horses? Speak well of them, varletto.[1]

*Bardolph:* Run away with the cozeners:[2] for so soon as I came beyond Eton, they threw me off from behind one of them, in a slough of mire,[3] and set spurs and away, like three German devils …

[1] *give me good news, you rascal*
[2] *cheats, con men*
[3] *muddy bog*

Doubt is cast on Bardolph's account when Sir Hugh and Caius – who had both sworn to take revenge on the host for thwarting their duel – run into the Garter one after the other.

First comes the parson, warning the host that he has heard a rumour about a trio of German fraudsters who have stolen horses and money from inns in the vicinity. Sir Hugh claims that he is passing on the report as a friendly gesture. After all, he remarks pointedly, the host is known for his judgement and his good humour:

*Evans:* I tell you for good will, look you: you are wise, and full of gibes and vlouting-stocks,[1] and 'tis not convenient you should be cozened.[2] Fare you well.

[1] *forever telling jokes and making laughing stocks of people*
[2] *tricked, cheated*

No sooner has the parson gone than the doctor hurries in. He too has a message, and like Evans he claims to be motivated by concern for the host. From his knowledge of the court, he can report that the German duke that the host has mentioned does not exist:

> *Caius:* ... it is tell-a me [1] dat you make grand preparation for a Duke de Jarmany. By my trot,[2] der is no Duke that the court is know to come. By gar, I tell you for good will. Adieu.
>
> [1] *I am told*
> [2] *in truth; I swear*

In a state of panic, the host runs out into the street, shouting at the top of his voice, hoping desperately to track down the thieves.

## Temptation

Falstaff is too troubled by his own misfortunes to feel any sympathy with the host. If his aristocratic friends heard about his soaking in the Thames or his battering at the hands of Master Ford, he would become an object of ridicule:

> *Falstaff:* If it should come to the ear of the court how I have been transformed,[1] and how my transformation hath been washed and cudgelled, they would melt me out of my fat drop by drop [2] ... I warrant they would whip me with their fine wits till I were as crestfallen as a dried pear.
>
> [1] *disguised, mistreated*
> [2] *my status would be reduced to nothing*

Mistress Quickly now comes into the Garter Inn. When Falstaff hears that she brings news from the two wives, he flatly refuses to have anything more to do with them. Mistress Quickly begs him to listen: the two women were not responsible for Falstaff's thrashing, she explains. Indeed, Mistress Ford has also been punished by her suspicious husband. Falstaff is unimpressed:

> *Falstaff:* I have suffered more for their sakes, more than the villainous inconstancy of man's disposition [1] is able to bear.
> *Mistress Quickly:* And have not they suffered? Yes, I warrant, speciously [2] one of them. Mistress Ford, good heart,

|  | is beaten black and blue, that[3] you cannot see a white spot about her. |
|---|---|
| *Falstaff:* | What tell'st thou me of black and blue? I was beaten myself into all the colours of the rainbow ... |

[1] *the terrible unreliability of human nature*
[2] *specially*
[3] *with the result that*

Mistress Quickly persists: despite everything, the women are still very keen to arrange a romantic rendezvous with him. She reveals that she has a letter that they have asked her to pass on. Unable to resist, Falstaff invites Mistress Quickly up to his room: he is ready to discuss the details of yet another meeting.

---

Throughout his long and successful career, the composer Giuseppe Verdi was renowned for his stirring, monumental operas. He was a great admirer of Shakespeare, and had created masterpieces based on the tragedies *Macbeth* and *Othello.* In his late seventies, however, he longed to write a comic opera, declaring that "after having relentlessly massacred so many heroes and heroines, I have at last the right to laugh a little."

In response, the writer Arrigo Boito, Verdi's collaborator and thirty years his junior, secretly started work on an adaptation of *The Merry Wives of Windsor*, hoping that the composer would agree to develop it into an opera. When Boito showed Verdi a draft of his text, the older man was hesitant: would he have the energy to write a full score at his age? Would he even live to see it performed? Eventually, however, he could not resist the opportunity, and three years later the opera *Falstaff* was complete.

The first night of *Falstaff*, at La Scala in Milan, was a triumph. The house was full to overflowing, with tickets selling at thirty times their normal price; Verdi himself was present, and when the performance was over, the rapturous applause for the singers, the musicians and the composer, by now 80 years old, lasted for over an hour.

# The host takes Fenton's side

A little while later, the host returns to the Garter, in the company of young Fenton. There is no sign of the stolen horses, and the host is in low spirits. His mood brightens a little, however, when Fenton makes him an offer.

The young gentleman is hoping to marry Anne Page, and he wants the host – who is known to favour the match – to help him. In return, Fenton promises to compensate him for the loss of his horses, and more:

| | |
|---|---|
| *Host:* | Master Fenton, talk not to me: my mind is heavy – I will give over all.[1] |
| *Fenton:* | Yet hear me speak. Assist me in my purpose, And, as I am a gentleman, I'll give thee A hundred pound in gold more than your loss. |

[1] *I'll have nothing more to do with your plans*

The host promises to listen, and not to reveal Fenton's proposal to anyone else. The young man starts by reminding the host how much he loves Anne, and how she feels the same about him. He then describes the events that have been planned for tonight around Herne's oak, when Falstaff will be mobbed by a group of children disguised as fairies before being confronted by the citizens of Windsor. Anne is to play the part of Fairy Queen.

Anne has told Fenton of her parents' plans for her marriage. Her father has explained that Slender will approach her tonight at a suitable moment: they are then to hurry away together, and must not stop until they reach Eton, where their wedding will take place. Like all the fairies, Anne will be wearing a mask; however, Slender will recognise her as she will be wearing a white costume.

Anne has told her father that she will go along with his scheme. However, she has also promised to follow her mother's wishes. Mistress Page has told doctor Caius to steal away with Anne – who will be dressed in green – when the opportunity arises. The couple will then make their way to a nearby chapel where a priest will be ready and waiting.

The host points out that Anne cannot please both her parents. In reply, Fenton explains that yet another vicar, and another church, must be prepared for a wedding soon after midnight tonight. The host promises to ensure that everything is in place for Fenton's marriage to Anne Page:

*Host:*      Which means she to deceive, father or mother?
*Fenton:*    Both, my good host, to go along with me.
              And here it rests:[1] that you'll procure the vicar
              To stay[2] for me at church, 'twixt twelve and one,
              And, in the lawful name of marrying,
              To give our hearts united ceremony.[3]
*Host:*      Well, husband your device;[4] I'll to the vicar.
              Bring you the maid, you shall not lack a priest.

[1] *this is the point; this is where I need your help*
[2] *wait*
[3] *unite us with the formal rites of marriage*
[4] *manage your plan carefully*

Fenton again promises to reward the host generously. Both men, their spirits raised, set off to prepare for the night's festivities.

---

*"Whether or not Elizabeth I commissioned* The Merry Wives of Windsor, *another queen – an empress, indeed – had an undoubted fondness for the play. Catherine the Great translated it into Russian in 1786 ... The scene was switched to St Petersburg; the characters were given Russian names – Justice Shallow became Shalov, Mistress Ford became Fordova; Falstaff was turned into a dandy who has come back from his travels abroad and is mocked for his Frenchified ways."*

John Gross, *After Shakespeare*, 2002

# Anticipation

Mistress Quickly has persuaded Falstaff, with the help of the letter from Mistresses Ford and Page, that his desires will finally be satisfied if he comes to meet the two women in Windsor Park tonight. They have asked him to come in the guise of the mythical Herne the Hunter, with majestic antlers on his head and brandishing ghostly chains.

Falstaff urges the talkative go-between to hurry back to the women with his reply. As she leaves, Mistress Quickly offers to help with his costume:

| | |
|---|---|
| *Falstaff:* | Prithee, no more prattling. Go, I'll hold:[1] this is the third time – I hope good luck lies in odd numbers. Away, go! They say there is divinity in odd numbers, either in nativity, chance or death.[2] Away! |
| *Mistress Quickly:* | I'll provide you a chain, and I'll do what I can to get you a pair of horns. |

[1] *keep the appointment*
[2] *odd numbers have divine powers, whether in matters of birth, adventure or death*

Just as Mistress Quickly leaves, another visitor comes to the Garter. It is Brook, who is keen to know how Sir John's pursuit of Mistress Ford is progressing. Falstaff reports that he has again been unlucky; her jealous husband came home unexpectedly and gave him a severe beating. If he had not been dressed as a woman, he claims, he would have fought back fearlessly:

| | |
|---|---|
| *Falstaff:* | That same knave, Ford her husband, hath the finest mad devil of jealousy in him, Master Brook, that ever governed frenzy.[1] I will tell you he beat me grievously, in the shape of a woman; for in the shape of man, Master Brook, I fear not Goliath with a weaver's beam[2] … |

[1] *is possessed by a jealous demon as wild as any that ever held power over a madman*
[2] *wielding a massive club*

Falstaff will have his revenge on Ford tonight, when he will at last seduce his wife; and then, he promises, the lady will no longer be able to resist Master Brook's advances.

## Master Page's plan
V, ii

It is late in the evening. Master Page is approaching Windsor Park in preparation for the midnight confrontation with Falstaff. With him is his prospective son-in-law Slender and Justice Shallow.

They have agreed that Slender, during the commotion of the night's events, should approach Anne – who will be wearing a white costume – and slip away with her for a night-time wedding. Page is about to remind him of the plan, but the young man has already made sure that he and Anne will be able to pick one another out in the crowd:

*Page:*     Remember, son Slender, my daughter –
*Slender:*  Ay, forsooth, I have spoke with her and we have a
            nay-word[1] how to know one another. I come to her
            in white, and cry 'mum'; she cries 'budget'; [2] and by
            that we know one another.

[1] *password*
[2] *'mumbudget' was a children's word meaning 'keep quiet'*

As they make their way towards the park, Page remarks that giving Falstaff his just deserts will be a pleasure. However, there is no malice involved in punishing the old rogue, who will provide quite a spectacle with antlers on his head:

*Page:*     God prosper our sport.[1] No man means evil but the
            devil, and we shall know him by his horns. Let's away;
            follow me.

[1] *may God ensure that our entertainment is a success*

The two wives, meanwhile, are also making their way to the park. Doctor Caius is with them, and Mistress Page encourages him to seize this opportunity to marry her daughter. He will recognise his bride-to-be, she reminds him, as the girl will be dressed in green. She sends him ahead, towards Windsor Park, urging him to sneak away with Anne when the time is right.

When her husband hears about the marriage, Mistress Page reflects, he will be displeased; it may even spoil his enjoyment at seeing Falstaff punished. This is a small price to pay, however, for preventing Anne's marriage to Slender:

*Mistress Page:* ... when you see your time, take her by the hand,
away with her to the deanery and dispatch it[1] quickly.
Go before into the park. – We two[2] must go together.
*Caius:* I know vat I have to do. Adieu. [*exit*]
*Mistress Page:* Fare you well, sir. – My husband will not rejoice
so much at the abuse of Falstaff as he will chafe[3] at
the Doctor's marrying my daughter. But 'tis no matter:
better a little chiding than a great deal of heartache.

[1] *get the wedding done*
[2] *Mistress Page and Mistress Ford*
[3] *be angry and exasperated*

The women discuss preparations for the coming night. The parson, disguised as a mischievous demon, is with the children in their fairy costumes and masks, led by Anne, the fairy queen: they are to hide in a hollow near Herne's oak, ready to jump out, their candles alight, as soon as Falstaff encounters the two women. Like her husband, Mistress Page is confident that playing tricks on a debauched character like Falstaff is perfectly justifiable:

*Mistress Ford:* We'll betray[1] him finely.
*Mistress Page:* Against such lewdsters[2] and their lechery
Those that betray them do no treachery.

[1] *deceive, hoodwink*
[2] *degenerates*

# The fairies assemble

It is nearly midnight. Out in Windsor Park, Sir Hugh is encouraging his young charges, in their fairy costumes, to remember the roles that they have rehearsed. It is time to go down into the hollow, he tells them, and wait for the arrival of their victim:

Evans:     Come, and remember your parts: be pold,[1] I pray you, follow me into the pit, and when I give the watch-'ords,[2] do as I pid[3] you. Come, come, trib,[4] trib.

[1] *bold*
[2] *password, signal*
[3] *bid*
[4] *trip, run nimbly*

# The love god

Falstaff is approaching Herne's oak. A distant bell has just chimed twelve, and Falstaff, resplendent in his stag's antlers, feels a mounting sense of excitement. He recalls how, according to ancient mythology, the mighty king of the gods would visit humanity in animal form in order to seduce his prey. He is very much in the same situation, he muses:

Falstaff:     Now the hot-blooded gods assist me! Remember, Jove, thou wast a bull for thy Europa:[1] love set on thy horns.[2] O powerful love, that in some respects makes a beast a man, in some other a man a beast! … When gods have hot backs,[3] what shall poor men do? For me, I am here a Windsor stag, and the fattest, I think, i'the forest.

[1] *a mythological princess abducted by the god Zeus, who took the form of a bull*
[2] *it was love that persuaded you to wear horns*
[3] *are lustful*

Mistress Ford calls out through the darkness, and Falstaff reaches out eagerly to find her. He is delighted to hear that she has company; he will happily satisfy both women. Clearly the god of love is making amends for his previous ill-treatment:

*Mistress Ford:* Mistress Page is come with me, sweetheart.

*Falstaff:* Divide me like a bribed buck, each a haunch.[1] … Speak I like Herne the Hunter? Why, now is Cupid a child of conscience:[2] he makes restitution. As I am a true spirit, welcome!

[1] *share me like a stolen deer, each taking a thigh and buttock*
[2] *a dutiful child*

Falstaff's advances are interrupted by the sudden blare of nearby hunting-horns. The two women run off, leaving Falstaff seething with frustration. He wonders whether the punishment he might expect in the next world is being meted out in this life instead:

*Falstaff:* I think the devil will not have me damned, lest the oil that's in me should set hell on fire; he would never else cross me thus.[1]

[1] *otherwise he would never thwart me like this*

## Retribution

Sir Hugh now leads his troupe of children out of their hiding place and towards Herne's oak. The children are masked and wearing fairy costumes, while the parson himself is disguised as an outlandish woodland creature. Among the fairies are Anne Page and Mistress Quickly, also disguised: and Pistol, previously one of Falstaff's followers, has come in the guise of the mischievous demon Hobgoblin.

The sudden appearance of this band of eerie forest folk, all illuminated by candlelight, throws Falstaff into a panic. Any mortal who witnesses the activities of spirits like these will die, he believes. He hurls himself to the ground, hiding his face:

*Falstaff:* They are fairies, he that speaks to them shall die. I'll wink and couch:[1] no man their work must eye.

[1] *close my eyes and lie down*

The spirits, chanting their rehearsed lines, prepare to go about their night-time deeds. Some are to inflict aches and pains on those mortals who have been thoughtless or disobedient, while the virtuous are to be granted sound sleep and sweet dreams. Other fairies are to roam through nearby Windsor Castle, home to the Queen, to spread good luck through the rooms and to make fairy rings of grass and flowers in the gardens.

Before the fairies set out on their nightly duties, they must carry out their traditional dance around Herne's oak. At this point, however, they sense an unwanted presence:

*Mistress Quickly:* ... Our dance of custom round about the oak
Of Herne the Hunter let us not forget.
*Evans:* Pray you, lock hand in hand, yourselves in order set;
And twenty glow-worms shall our lanterns be
To guide our measure [1] round about the tree.
But stay [2] – I smell a man of middle earth. [3]

[1] *steps, dance*
[2] *stop, wait*
[3] *mortal, human being; one who lives on earth,
between heaven and hell*

The woodland spirits confront the terrified Falstaff. He must be subjected to a trial, they declare. If he feels pain at the touch of a burning candle, it is a sign of a wicked, dissolute character. The result is inevitable:

*Pistol:* Vile worm, thou wast o'erlooked [1] even in thy birth.
*Mistress Quickly:* With trial fire touch me [2] his finger end:
If he be chaste, the flame will back descend
And turn him to no pain; but if he start, [3]
It is the flesh of a corrupted heart.
*Pistol:* A trial, come.
*Evans:* Come, will this wood [4] take fire?
[*they burn him with their candles*]
*Falstaff:* Oh, oh, oh!
*Mistress Quickly:* Corrupt, corrupt, and tainted in desire!

[1] *looked on with an evil eye, put under a spell*
[2] *for me*
[3] *reacts, flinches*
[4] *this finger*

*... twenty glow-worms shall our lanterns be*
*To guide our measure round about the tree.*

The appearance of the fairies marks a sudden change in the play. The conversational prose gives way to ceremonial verse, and for a brief interval an atmosphere of solemnity and ritual prevails.

In 1597 Lord Hunsdon, patron of Shakespeare's acting company, was made a Knight of the Garter. It seems likely that this scene was performed as part of the celebrations following this event: in fact the whole play may have been written with this occasion in mind, given that one of its most significant locations is named the Garter Inn:

*"The switch to verse signals a different kind of drama. The play has at this point become a masque – a stylized, courtly form of entertainment involving elaborate sets, declamatory poetry and courtly audience participation for complex and lengthy dances ... The Merry Wives of Windsor itself may well have been performed before Elizabeth and her knights on St George's Day 1597, as a celebration of the annual feast of the Order of the Garter, as well as being staged in the public theatre for a completely different audience."*

Catherine Richardson, Introduction to the Penguin edition of *The Merry Wives of Windsor*, 2005

The fairies now surround Falstaff, pinching him mercilessly as they recite their lines, reprimanding him for his wickedness. As he struggles to fend them off, crying out in pain, they threaten to torment him all night:

| *Children:* | Fie on[1] sinful fantasy, |
| | Fie on lust and luxury![2] |
| | Lust is but a bloody fire, |
| | Kindled with unchaste desire ... |

[1] *away with, down with*
[2] *debauchery*

Amidst the uproar, three of the fairies are snatched away by bystanders: one dressed in white is taken by Slender, one in green is picked out by doctor Caius, and a third runs off with Fenton.

A moment later, the sound of a hunting horn is heard again, and the fairies scatter into the night. Falstaff, battered, bruised and scorched, is left lying under Herne's oak.

## Telling the truth

Falstaff eventually gathers the strength to stand up. Aching and dejected, he removes his antlers and starts to set off back to the town. At this point, however, the two wives return to the scene, along with their husbands. Picking up the horns, they make no attempt to hide their amusement at Falstaff's predicament.

Master Ford mimics the knight's voice as he imagines a conversation with the enigmatic Master Brook. Ford reveals, at the same time, that he intends to get back the money that he gave to Falstaff when he was playing the part of Brook:

*Ford:*  Here are his horns, Master Brook. And, Master Brook, he hath enjoyed nothing of Ford's but his buck-basket,[1] his cudgel and twenty pounds of money, which must be paid to Master Brook. His horses are arrested [2] for it, Master Brook.

[1] *laundry basket*
[2] *confiscated, impounded until the money is repaid*

Mistress Ford, too, cannot resist a pun at the fat knight's expense, while pretending to lament their doomed love affair. Falstaff finally begins to accept that his plans have failed utterly:

*Mistress Ford:*  Sir John, we have had ill luck, we could never meet. I will never take you for my love again, but I will always count you my deer.
*Falstaff:*  I do begin to perceive that I am made an ass.

It dawns on Falstaff that the creatures that were tormenting him just now were not fairies after all. The parson, no longer playing the role of a spirit of the forest, rebukes Falstaff for his depravity. He admonishes Ford, too, who teases Sir Hugh for his impenetrable Welsh accent:

*Evans:* Sir John Falstaff, serve Got,[1] and leave your desires, and fairies will not pinse [2] you.
*Ford:* Well said, fairy Hugh.
*Evans:* And leave you your jealousies too, I pray you.
*Ford:* I will never mistrust my wife again, till thou art able to woo her in good English.

[1] *God*
[2] *pinch*

Falstaff bitterly regrets his folly in imagining that he might succeed in seducing the two wives and helping himself to their husbands' money. Mistress Page agrees that he has been utterly deluded: even if she and her friend lost all their inhibitions, what would they see in him? The others drive the point home enthusiastically:

*Mistress Page:* Why, Sir John, do you think, though we would have thrust virtue out of our hearts by the head and shoulders, and have given ourselves without scruple to hell,[1] that ever the devil could have made you our delight?
*Ford:* What, a hodge-pudding? [2] A bag of flax? [3]
*Mistress Page:* A puffed man?
*Page:* Old, cold, withered and of intolerable entrails? [4]
*Ford:* And one that is as slanderous as Satan?
*Page:* And as poor as Job? [5]

[1] *even if we had removed any trace of morality from our hearts, and had willingly accepted eternal damnation*
[2] *pudding made from a mix of assorted ingredients*
[3] *sack stuffed with raw fibres*
[4] *with an excessively large paunch*
[5] *biblical character who lost all his wealth*

> *... till thou art able to woo her in good English.*
>
> *"Whatever the occasion that suggested it, Shakespeare made* Merry Wives *into a joyous exploration of the main tool of his trade, the English language ... In fact* Merry Wives *is not so much an 'English comedy' as 'the Comedy of English', or rather 'the Comedy of Language'. In no other Shakespearean play does the word 'English' with reference to the language and its misuse appear so frequently."*
>
> Giorgio Melchiori, Introduction to the Arden edition of *The Merry Wives of Windsor*, 2000

Falstaff, resigned to the fact that he has become an object of ridicule, does not attempt to defend himself. He agrees to return with the citizens to Windsor, where he will repay the money gained illicitly from Master Brook.

The mood lightens when Page invites Falstaff to his home for a nightcap. Sir John will not be the only figure of fun, promises Page. When his wife learns about their daughter's marriage, her reaction will be worth seeing:

*Page:*  Yet be cheerful, knight: thou shalt eat a posset[1] tonight at my house, where I will desire thee to laugh at my wife that now laughs at thee. Tell her Master Slender hath married her daughter.

[1] *hot drink made with milk, spices and liquor*

Mistress Page is untroubled, quietly confident that she has foiled her husband's plans for Anne:

*Mistress Page:* [*aside*] ... if Anne Page be my daughter, she is, by this,[1] Doctor Caius' wife.

[1] *by now, by this time*

# Harmony restored

Slender now comes back to join the assembled citizens. Page greets his new son-in-law warmly, but the young man's response is furious:

*Slender:* I came yonder at Eton to marry Mistress Anne Page – and she's a great lubberly[1] boy! If it had not been i'the church, I would have swinged[2] him ...

[1] *rough, uncouth*
[2] *thumped*

Master Page is baffled: he had carefully explained that his daughter was the fairy dressed all in white. Slender retorts that the mistake was not his: he even used their agreed password. Page's wife cuts in gently, explaining that she was responsible for the misunderstanding:

*Slender:* I went to her in white, and cried 'mum', and she cried 'budget', as Anne and I had appointed.[1] And yet it was not Anne, but a postmaster's boy.[2]
*Mistress Page:* Good George, be not angry: I knew of your purpose, turned[3] my daughter into green, and indeed she is now with the doctor at the deanery, and there married.

[1] *arranged*
[2] *stable-boy*
[3] *changed*

Doctor Caius appears on the scene just as his name is mentioned. Like Slender, he is extremely irate, having discovered that his partner was not the woman he expected, even though he chose the fairy wearing green as agreed. Ford poses the obvious question:

*Caius:* Vere is Mistress Page? By gar, I am cozened.[1] I ha' married *un garçon*, a boy, *un paysan*,[2] by gar! A boy it is not Anne Page. By gar, I am cozened.
*Mistress Page:* Why, did you take her in green?
*Caius:* Ay, by gar, and 'tis a boy! By gar, I'll raise[3] all Windsor.

*Ford:* This is strange. Who hath got the right Anne?

[1] *cheated, swindled*
[2] *peasant, yokel*
[3] *rouse, call to arms*

Right on cue, Fenton now arrives, alongside his new wife, Anne Page. Anne's parents angrily demand to know why she did not marry either of the men that they had chosen for her.

Fenton defends their union passionately. The two of them have been in love for a long time, and to marry her forcibly to another man would be a sin. Their love has now been sanctified in the marriage vows which they have just entered into:

*Fenton:* Hear the truth of it:
You would have married her most shamefully
Where there was no proportion held in love.[1]
The truth is, she and I, long since contracted,[2]
Are now so sure[3] that nothing can dissolve us.
Th'offence is holy that she hath committed ...

[1] *where the two partners did not love one another
    equally*
[2] *betrothed, promised to each other*
[3] *firmly united*

---

*... she's a great lubberly boy!*

Acting companies in Elizabethan England were exclusively male; all the women's roles were played by young boys. Given this limitation, Shakespeare seems to have enjoyed teasing his audience with the resulting opportunities for gender confusion. So just as Caius and Slender were taken in by their sham brides, his audience too had been fooled into accepting Anne Page as a young woman:

*"The boy gets the girl, just as the audience would want; at the same time Shakespeare reminds them that they have been wilfully deceived into precisely the same falsehood accepted by two of the play's most foolish characters."*

SparkNotes Editors, Commentary on *The Merry Wives of Windsor*, 2005

---

Ford turns to the Pages. They have no choice but to accept what has happened, he advises. Love cannot be imposed or controlled, but must be left to take its true course:

Ford:     Stand not amazed,[1] here is no remedy.
          In love the heavens themselves do guide the state.[2]
          Money buys lands, but wives are sold by fate.

          [1] *don't look so shocked*
          [2] *govern human affairs*

Falstaff is pleased to find that he is not the only person who has been deceived; the very people who schemed against him have themselves been fooled. It takes only a matter of moments, however, for Master and Mistress Page to become reconciled to the new state of affairs. All is forgiven, they declare, both Falstaff's plot and their daughter's secret marriage:

Falstaff:     I am glad, though you have ta'en a special stand to
              strike at me, that your arrow hath glanced.[1]
Page:         Well, what remedy? Fenton, God give thee joy!
              What cannot be eschewed[2] must be embraced.
Falstaff:     When night-dogs run, all sorts of deer are chased.[3]
Mistress Page: Well, I will muse[4] no further. – Master Fenton,
              God give you many, many merry days!

              [1] *though you have taken great care to choose a place
              from which to shoot, your arrow has not pierced its
              target*
              [2] *avoided*
              [3] *dogs that hunt at night are likely to catch unexpected
              prey*
              [4] *wonder, complain*

The party heads back to Windsor in high spirits. It is time for all of them – Falstaff included – to go home, sit round a warm fire and laugh over all their recent escapades. Ford reminds Sir John of his strange visitor, Master Brook, and his determination to seduce Ford's wife. It is now clear that, as Falstaff promised, Master Brook will be satisfied:

*Mistress Page:* ... let us every one go home,
And laugh this sport o'er by a country fire,
Sir John and all.
*Ford:* Let it be so, Sir John.
To Master Brook you yet shall hold your word,
For he tonight shall lie with Mistress Ford.

———

Even those critics who do not hold *The Merry Wives of Windsor* in high esteem will generally concede that it has always been, and remains, universally popular:

*"The conduct of this drama is deficient ... but its general power, that power by which all works of genius shall finally be tried, is such that perhaps it never yet had reader or spectator who did not think it too soon at an end."*

Dr Johnson, *The Plays of William Shakespeare*, 1765

# Acknowledgements

The following publications have proved invaluable as sources of factual information and critical insight:

- Jonathan Bate, Introduction to the RSC Shakespeare edition of *The Merry Wives of Windsor*, Macmillan, 2011

- Jonathan Bate, *Soul of the Age*, Penguin, 2009

- Harold Bloom, *Shakespeare: The Invention of the Human*, HarperCollins, 1998

- Charles Boyce, *Shakespeare A to Z*, Roundtable Press, 1990

- Walter Cohen, Introduction to the Norton Shakespeare edition of *The Merry Wives of Windsor*, 1977

- Kathy Elgin, Programme notes for the RSC production of *The Merry Wives of Windsor*, Royal Shakespeare Theatre, 1992

- Alison Findlay, *Women in Shakespeare*, Bloomsbury, 2014

- Nicholas Fogg, *Hidden Shakespeare*, Amberley, 2013

- John Gross, *After Shakespeare*, Oxford University Press, 2002

- G. R. Hibbard, Commentary on the Penguin Classics edition of *The Merry Wives of Windsor*, 1973

- Laurie Maguire and Emma Smith, *30 Great Myths about Shakespeare*, Wiley-Blackwell, 2013

- Giorgio Melchiori, Introduction to the Arden Shakespeare edition of *The Merry Wives of Windsor*, Bloomsbury, 2000

- Catherine Richardson, Introduction to the Penguin Classics edition of *The Merry Wives of Windsor*, 2005

- SparkNotes Editors, Commentary on *The Merry Wives of Windsor*, sparknotes.com/shakespeare/merrywives/section9, SparkNotes LLC, 2005

- A.W. Ward and A. R. Waller, *The Cambridge History of English and American Literature*, Cambridge University Press, 1921

- Michael Wood, *In Search of Shakespeare*, BBC Books, 2005

Guides currently available in the *Shakespeare Handbooks* series are:

- **Antony & Cleopatra** (ISBN 978 1 899747 02 3)
- **As You Like It** (ISBN 978 1 899747 00 9)
- **The Comedy of Errors** (ISBN 978 1 899747 16 0)
- **Cymbeline** (ISBN 978 1 899747 20 7)
- **Hamlet** (ISBN 978 1 899747 07 8)
- **Henry IV, Part 1** (ISBN 978 1 899747 05 4)
- **Julius Caesar** (ISBN 978 1 899747 11 5)
- **King Lear** (ISBN 978 1 899747 03 0)
- **Macbeth** (ISBN 978 1 899747 04 7)
- **Measure for Measure** (ISBN 978 1 899747 14 6)
- **The Merchant of Venice** (ISBN 978 1 899747 13 9)
- **The Merry Wives of Windsor** (ISBN 978 1 899747 18 4)
- **A Midsummer Night's Dream** (ISBN 978 1 899747 09 2)
- **Much Ado About Nothing** (ISBN 978 1 899747 17 7)
- **Othello** (ISBN 978 1 899747 12 2)
- **Richard II** (ISBN 978 1 899747 19 1)
- **Romeo & Juliet** (ISBN 978 1 899747 10 8)
- **The Tempest** (ISBN 978 1 899747 08 5)
- **Twelfth Night** (ISBN 978 1 899747 01 6)
- **The Winter's Tale** (ISBN 978 1 899747 15 3)

**www.shakespeare-handbooks.com**

Printed in Great Britain
by Amazon

38159063R00056